The Tebbit Test

The Tebbit Test

The Memoirs of a Cricketing Fanatic

Icki Iqbal

To Kadeeja, for her companionship and love

First published: 11.11.2011
ISBN No. 978-0-9570266-0-5

DDKM Publishing
Guadaleste, Sandy Way, Cobham, Surrey, KT11 2EY
Telephone: 01372 841881

Publishing consultant: Zoesbooks at www.zoesbooks.co.uk

Typeset in Garamond and French Script MT by
Helm Information
amandahelm@helm-information.co.uk
www.helm-information.co.uk

Printed and bound in Great Britain by
Berforts Group, Stevenage, SG1 2BH
www.berforts.co.uk

Contents

Foreword

When I picked up this book, I had very little inkling of what awaited me. Despite being informed by the author that I was going to read his autobiography interspersed with cricket, I was taken aback. One of the funniest books I have read in many a year, I was genuinely impressed by the quality of writing. If someone had said to me that a Pakistani Ramchandar Guha was waiting in the wings to establish his independent credentials, I would have scoffed at him. Yet here is a tale, written tongue-in-cheek, which gives the reader no warning of what awaits him in the final chapter. The final statements are as tragic as those of William Shakespeare writing on Hamlet, Prince of Denmark.

The ultimate question one need ask oneself is how can one judge a country in the third world with standards set for them by the Western World?

Pakistan's struggles continue, despite abuse from within and the same from without. Talent such as that of Hanif Mohammed, Fazal Mahmood, Imran Khan, Javed Miandad, Wasim Akram, Waqar Younus, Shoaib Akhtar, Saqlain Mushtaq, Inzamamul Haq and Mohammed Amir will resurrect Pakistan and its cricket, time and again as the author struggles to elaborate. The real problem will always be the decadence and corruption that governs the innocent and simple people of Pakistan. Perhaps patience, the will to fight and the belief in one's self will some day see its people through. Pakistan has not always chosen the right way forward, but faith can move mountains and so will the nation of Pakistan, if one continues to have faith in them.

Khadim Hussain Baloch
Author of *Encyclopaedia of Pakistan Cricket*

Foreword

Icki Iqbal has written a book which appeals to several audiences, but above all to those who have an affection for both the Indian sub-continent and cricket.

It is quite extraordinary that the game of cricket has put down its roots so deeply into many parts of the old British Empire, but deepest of all in places as unalike as Australiasia, India and Pakistan.

Born in 1945 in India, he was brought up in Pakistan; his father a Muslim and civil servant of the British Raj having migrated to Pakistan after independence and partition. The account of his childhood and the beginnings of his lifelong love affair with cricket speaks volumes not only about this intensely decent, humorous (and slightly mischevious) man, but also the complex relationship with Britain, or rather, England and the sub-continent. This is often described as one of both love and hate, but in my experience and certainly that of Icki Iqbal, there is far, far more love about it than hate.

He made a career in England as an actuary, rising to board level in a major subsidiary of a quoted public company, belying the old saw that actuaries are men who found accountancy too exciting, despite his difficulty in taking any part of life seriously except his family and cricket.

Always realistic, perhaps too modest about his abilities, Icki Iqbal realised early on that he was a cricket enthusiast rather than a player, and he would have surely been picked for either England or Pakistan's first XI of enthusiasts.

It has been a sadness for him that in recent times Pakistan particularly, but perhaps not Pakistan alone, has lost something of the spirit of cricket which he rightly sees as being as important as its laws. I think that is how he had come to feel himself as so settled into English ways that, without deserting his inheritance, he can feel comfortable about 'the cricket test'.

He has, in his words, married his 'mistress', English cricket.

This is a thoroughly good read, full of hard fact and wise opinions about both cricket and life. We should be happy to have Icki Iqbal on board.

Norman Tebbit

1. Genesis

My family migrated from India to Pakistan in March 1948 when I was three. By family, I mean my Mum and few months old sister. Dad, a Muslim in the Indian Civil Service who opted for Pakistan when partition came, had to up sticks quickly and move to Karachi, in September 1947.

A cousin of his accompanied us to Karachi and Dad was there to receive us. We lived in accommodation provided by the Government to its employees. The address was 40/4 Napier Barracks. Napier and Frere[1] were two key men who brought large tracts of India under British rule and Karachi was full of streets, roads and localities named after them. Napier Barracks were terraced houses designed for British Civil Servants and were spacious but Spartan. Every house had a veranda which was enclosed by a wooden wall that we called 'jaffery' and was like a wooden trellis (*see picture on page 7*). We were there until the spring of 1952, four years. The houses were set some hundred yards from the road, which was a main arterial road on bus routes. There was no grass in those hundred yards. My memory is of the colour beige so it was probably compacted sand. Certainly there was a lot of sand in Karachi.

It was in Karachi that I first saw big boys (i.e. those aged perhaps ten to twelve) playing cricket. Early in the evening when the sun was taking its ardour to other parts of the world, boys used to come with stumps, bat and ball and pitch up in the aforementioned hundred yards. The balls used to be tennis balls. On one occasion a lofted shot ended up in a neighbour's chimney. Don't ask me why the house had a chimney; perhaps it was for the kitchen.

We were a middle-class family. Dad had no assets as he'd left them all behind when he migrated. In any case he was under thirty. But he

---

1.   Frere, who had a conscience, after one victory sent a famous telegram, a single word pun 'Paccavi' which is Latin for 'I have sinned', i.e. 'I have Sindh'.

had a decent middle-class income and, as was common then, we had a cook and a teenaged help. But the term middle class covers a very wide spread. He sent his kids (there were five of us by 1954) to fee-paying schools, but we were usually less affluent than most in our class. We did not own a car until 1959 when Dad bought a seven-year-old Opel Olympia. He did not own a house until after I bought mine, although mine was on a 90% mortgage, his was paid for in cash.

When I was four I joined Arabic classes to learn to read the Qu'ran. It was held in our neighbour's house where a lady taught some half a dozen of us. She taught us the Arabic script and how to read the Qu'ran starting with the first chapter, which is very similar to the Christian Lord's Prayer, and then progressing through the entire book. By the time we left Karachi some three years later, I had just got to the end of the Holy Book. But it was parrot-fashion reading. I had no idea what the words meant. That came a decade later when, of my own volition, I read the translation Dad used.

Mum taught me the English alphabet and how to spell my name. She spelt it as Mohammed Iqbal. When I was five, Dad enrolled me in a Montessori School with a non-standard method of teaching. It was more like the stuff Brian Cant did on the BBC program *Play Away*. We didn't have formal learning of language or sums. Instead we had picture books and objects to name and count. That's as much as I remember. I'm not sure why Dad chose the school; perhaps he'd been recommended it or perhaps it was the only school which had a place for me. He enrolled me as Muhammad Iqbal. There are several different spellings of my first name and I guess each parent used the one that came naturally to them. It has led to confusion in adult life.

I have no idea where the school was. When I returned to Karachi in 1959, I could not locate it. It was a short bus-ride away from Napier Barracks and a teenaged help used to take me there and bring me back. He was under strict instruction to see me right into the school. After a while, a combination of his laziness and my desire to do the rest of the journey on my own, meant that he only saw me get off the bus and didn't see me to school. One day, when I got to the school I found it closed. I had to walk all the way back. I'm not sure how I remembered the route but I managed to get home in an hour or so. Mum was horrified at what might have happened on the way.

The language used in every-day life was Urdu and Mum and Dad

Father holding my brother Rehman; my sister Mariam is on the left.

didn't know it. Their mother tongue was Malayalam. Whilst we were in Karachi they spoke to me in Malayalam. Urdu script was the same as Arabic, i.e. it was Persian. But the words were alien to them[2]. So they had to learn it by listening. One problem was that, in Urdu, inanimate objects had gender. There were no rules and no short cuts. You just had to learn by rote. By 1955 Mum's Urdu was fairly fluent, if you ignored her problems with gender, and she spoke to me in it. Dad switched to English as he never really mastered Urdu. As for me, because I studied in English-medium schools and all the stuff – books and magazines – I read was in English, English is now my first language, Urdu a poor second and Malayalam an also-ran. Those who're familiar with my English might wonder what that says about my knowledge of the

2. When the Moguls ruled India in the 17th and 18th century, the court language was Persian whilst the natives spoke Hindi. The soldiers and courtiers who had to deal with the local population developed a hybrid: essentially Hindi but with Persian words thrown in and using Persian script. That is the origin of Urdu. Some 80–90% of the words in Urdu and Hindi are the same but both contain words that the other language does not; Urdu contains Persian words and Hindi Sanskrit words. Thus Indians and Pakistanis can speak to each other but cannot write to each other as the scripts are different.

other two languages. The answer is 'everything'. I'm no linguist. (All the more surprising that my daughter is fluent in English, French, Italian and Russian, my son in English, Spanish and Italian and my wife in Malayalam, English and Italian). However I digress.

Kids pick up new languages faster than adults so I was ahead of my parents. I also learnt a few swear words. I didn't know what they meant but had an instinctive feeling that the words were taboo.

There must have been a number of young families as, in the evening, a large number of young boys and girls used to assemble to play all sorts of games. Our next door neighbour had a son my age and a daughter two years older. She was naturally bossy and led in all the games we played in. I mixed with all but was, to some extent, an outsider as my Urdu wasn't fluent. One day, keen to show some guts, I used a swear word. The bossy girl said, 'Ooooo, he's rude let's get him.' She then chased me and all the other kids followed. We ran the length of the ground in front of our houses in a single file, me first and then the others shouting, 'Get him'. I ran into Mum's arm and the bossy girl told her, 'He's being rude.' Mum didn't understand a word and the kids eventually left. I was whimpering and I got a cuddle and kiss from Mum. A shy woman, not known for public displays of affection – that was the last time she kissed me.

In 1952, Dad got transferred to Bahawalpur. We spent a year there before Dad got transferred to Lahore and then a year later, in 1954, to Rawalpindi. That is where this story begins. I was nine.

We rented one-half of a very basic house. We used to call it a hut. Its party walls were made of cardboard – or so it seemed to me – but probably plasterboard. In the other half was the family of a work colleague of Dad's. He had a younger brother who became a good friend even though he was fourteen and I, nine.

My seven-year-old sister obstinately refused to join school. In order to placate her, instead of putting me in St Mary's, the boys' school Dad had intended me to join, I was put in the school my sister was trying to avoid. Presentation Convent accepted boys in the primary school. We had a Mother Superior who was a ferocious disciplinarian. Most of the boys in my class were aged ten and naturally boisterous. If any was found talking when Mother Superior entered he would be caned on his backside. Sitting in the back row, I found it amusing to see these ostensibly butch boys screaming in pain. One day Mother Superior spotted this and said:

'So you think this is funny, do you, Iqbal? Let's see if you will still laugh after this,' as she proceeded to cane me. I was a skinny lad and cane on bone is extremely painful. As a matter of pride I showed no pain even though it was hurting like hell. It dawned on me that she'd just carry on caning me with increasing vigour. The other lads knew what they were doing, when they grimaced. So I let out a wail and a few seconds after that, caning ceased.

17th August 1954 was the day I first became interested in cricket. My neighbour's younger brother came running into our house shouting, 'We've done it, we've done it, we've beaten England'. Dad, never really interested in sport, was equally jubilant. It was just the sort of fillip a young nation needed. Adults were still in awe of our former colonial masters and beating England was especially sweet to them. The victory generated widespread interest in schools in the cities. I was hooked.

Adjacent to our hut was a large house in a plot of perhaps one acre. It was rented by an army colonel who had a son of my age and I often played cricket with him. There was only one snag: he had an older sister. Girls mature faster than boys anyway and there's a massive difference between a twelve-year-old girl and nine-year-old boy. She bossed her brother and me. We both hated her. Why? Because she'd do all the batting and, as she acted as the *de facto* umpire, we could never get her out. In an act of defiance, we made a rule that only boys could play cricket. So she cut her hair short and wore shorts and looked every inch a boy. I was not fooled and said to her, 'You can't fool us. Underneath you're a girl.'

'No I'm not.'

'Yes you are.'

'No, I'm *not*.'

'Yes, you are' said her brother. 'You don't have a willy, just a crack.'

'You're rude. I'm going to tell Dad.'

'You started it.'

This had become a sibling quarrel that only they could settle. But she decided to bide her time, possibly until their mum and dad arrived. Instead she turned her attention to me. She had one trump card that I was powerless against; her dad had bought all the gear; I had none. I was banned.

The following year, 1955, I moved to St Mary's and stayed there until

17th August 1954, the run-out that transformed my life. Pakistan win at the Oval and square the series. Note that the umpire hasn't moved to be in position to adjudicate the run out. If you click on 'Fazal Mahmood cricketer' on Youtube you will see precious footage of this event. Aside from the hilarity of hearing Hafeez Kardar speak like an Englishman, it is astonishing to see how muted the celebrations were; a bit like Manchester 1956 after Jim Laker's ten/nineteen wicket haul. How times change.

the summer of 1958. A school bus picked me up and the journey took forty-five minutes. The prospectus stated that the school was run by 'Fathers from Mill Hill, London'. They were certainly many Catholic priests from England and Ireland (Byrne, McCann, etc.).

Most of the teaching staff were native Pakistanis; some career teachers, some marking time until a better job came along. Two teachers stand out in my memory. One was Mrs Lobo, a very attractive Goan, with whom all the teenage boys were in love. The other was a Mr Rogers who taught the fourth and fifth forms English, Maths and Science and prepared them for the public exam conducted on behalf of Cambridge University.

Cricket was played in the school but, in my time, not by the school. Outside the Headmaster's Office, in the waiting room, there was a wooden board on which were etched the names of three students who'd been awarded school colours in 1953. Obtaining school colours must have been more special than playing in the first team, as there were only three names on it. Two of them were Javed Burki and Ijaz Butt.

However, in my time the school did not actively encourage cricket. There was no sports master or competitive sport. Sure, there were annual grudge matches against Burn Hall, a sister school in the hill station Abbotabad, but selection of the team was a last minute job.

Nevertheless the boys were cricket mad. Every break time was utilised and every contest mattered. Lacking hand-eye co-ordination and being unable to keep my eyes on the ball throughout its journey until it made contact with the bat, I was destined to peak at mediocrity. Whilst I was at St Mary's, I probably played in more matches than any other boy in my age group. I might have been no good but I was always available. Until I was thirteen we played without pads or gloves and we didn't know what a groin box was.

Being small for my age, opposing bowlers used to ease up on seeing me. I could never get the ball off the square but I could block. If I blocked for fifteen minutes, bowlers used to lose their patience and crank up their speed. I would always get into line but would take my eyes off the ball, so being hit on the body was not uncommon. Many a time I had taken yorkers on my toe which was covered by flimsy cloth trainers. I would smile through intense pain and contrive to miss a straight one. My other weaknesses were (a) I could not play the off or cover or square drive, my only strokes being the straight drive, a hoick to mid-wicket and the cut and the leg-glance and (b) fielding, at which I was hopeless.

What I could do was bowl. Off a short run up I bowled flat trajectory left-arm spin. I seldom turned the ball but I kept a good length. Most batsmen found me difficult to score off, but every now and then I would come across a half-decent batsman who would find my guileless predictability to his liking and I'd get punished.

I remember once connecting with a leg glance with such exquisite timing that the ball sped off the bat like a bullet. I was still bewitched by the beauty of the stroke when I was clean bowled next ball. I seldom got into double figures and my highest score ever was 39 but, truth be told, that was in a single-wicket contest, against my younger sister. My highest in a proper match was 20. As Glenn McGrath once said about batting at number eleven, 'No sooner have you got your eye in, the other guy gets out.'

No one wants to umpire but I often got lumbered with it, as I'd always be around but often not in the team. On one occasion, when my team was bowling and a ball hit the batsman's leg (and an unprotected one at that), I instinctively jumped up and down shouting *Howzat*, forgetting that I was the umpire. Concentration was a particular problem as I my mind was given to wander. One day, my mate who was bowling, noted that I wasn't watching and bellowed in my ear, 'Howzat'. My finger went up automatically before I knew what I'd done. I hadn't a clue whether he was out or not but I was too proud to retract my decision.

Actually, it is a simplification to suggest that *all* boys were cricket mad. A sizeable minority went for hockey, but I had no interest in it. I did try to play it once but, when I tried to dribble past someone, he hacked me down with such a savage blow that I lost all interest.

In 1956, when I was eleven, we moved to a larger (rented) house, 111 Murree Road. It was in the Cantonment area. St Mary's was also on Murree Road but was in the City area. I persuaded my parents that public transport was better than the school bus. I would pocket the bus fare and walk the distance, some forty-five minutes, so as to create funds to buy cricket magazines. Dad didn't believe in pocket money.

Although single-storey, as most houses in Rawalpindi were, this house was large enough to be rented out to two families. We were in one half of the house with a good acre of surrounding land in our half. A childless couple rented the other half. The rooms had high ceilings which was good in the summer. In the winter we used a small coal stove to keep us warm. For bathing, hot water was supplied in two buckets but had to be used quickly as it cooled rapidly. In the summer it was common practice to lock the house and sleep outside. We did this in the courtyard at the back. Although our neighbours were childless, at one stage his brother stayed for several months with his newly-married wife. I was twelve or thirteen by then and I could guess what they were up to making strange noises. It surprised me that they weren't embarrassed doing it within earshot of us and his elder brother.

The reader might be wondering how my parents coped. I never thought about it. Around that time, when we were learning the facts of life a mate said to me, 'You Dad must be doing it to your Mum.' I was so incensed at the suggestion that my parents would indulge in something as dirty as that, that I tried to beat him up. He was, however, much bigger than me and I got roundly thrashed instead. When I went home and Dad saw the cuts and bruises on my arms and legs, he gave me a stern lecture on the dangers of mixing with the wrong sort of people. What could I say? Sometimes kids know better than adults and just keep quiet.

As the house had a decent-sized lawn I used it as a cricket pitch. The grass was cut by a young lad using a scythe. We didn't pay him anything but he made money by collecting the clippings in a sack and selling it as horse food: tongas and Victorias being a common mode of transport. I formed a cricket team, collected membership fees to create the funds necessary to buy stumps, a bat and ball. I called the team 'Eaglets', the eagle being the emblem of the national team. Because it was 'my' ground, I appointed myself the captain. I was not a popular captain as I invariably lost the toss and had to field first. 'You're a useless tosser,' my team-mates might have said had they known cockney slang. The ground was actually not large enough to permit bowling from both ends. At the end of each over batsmen had to swap ends. Rather like batting with a runner, this often led to moments of confusion and hilarity.

Arshad Nassar who, with Javed Mahmood was my closest friend, opened the bowling. The other opening bowler was Lancelot Cross. Not only was Lancelot fast, by our standards, he was grateful to be picked. Why? He was the son of a lowly steam-engine driver whom other teams avoided. He was two years older than me and jet black in colour. His sister, Mary Cross, was in my class in my solitary year at Presentation

Convent. Javed Mahmood lived nearby and always played. Dilawar Mani and Ehsan Mani, brothers, turned out occasionally. Ehsan rose to be the head of the ICC, the body that presides over world cricket, and Dilawar is currently the Chairman of the Abu Dhabi Cricket Club. An English boy, Terence Leather (pronounced, Lee-ther, not as in the animal hide) also played.

A classmate who lived four miles away and had his own team, challenged us and a match was arranged at our ground on a Saturday afternoon. I won the toss and for some deeply tactical reason sent them in. They batted through the winter afternoon and scored a hundred odd. As our typical team total was sixty odd, we had a challenge on our hands. Before we could start our innings, my opposite number said that his team had to get home before dark but they'd return the next week to complete the match. They didn't. I suffered a lot of grief from my team.

Until the age of eleven I showed no interest in studies which caused my father much grief. It irritated him to see me devouring and retaining cricket news. He had two newspapers delivered to him; one a Pakistani daily (either *Dawn* or *Morning News*) and one an Indian one (*Statesman* to begin with, but later the *Indian Express*). The quality of reporting was best in the *Statesman*. It also, one year, serialised Len Hutton's autobiography, *Just My Story*. Like other boys, I collected cricket pictures cut out from newspapers and magazines. Kardar had written a book on the 1954 tour of England called *Test Status on Trial*. Most boys owned a copy but I didn't.

A market of sorts developed in trading cricket pictures. Nobody thought twice about cheating their best friend. In 1954/55, immediately after touring Australia (the Tyson tour), England had moved to New Zealand and played two Tests there, in one of which they'd got New Zealand all out for 26; yes folks, it is not a typo! Bert Sutcliffe had scored 73 in the first Test and a picture of him had appeared in the *Dawn* at a time when father was subscribing to the *Morning News*; or vice versa. A few months later, a friend came to do a swap and offered me a picture of Sutcliffe in return for three or four other pictures I cannot remember. He knew that I badly wanted the Sutcliffe. After the transaction was concluded he said triumphantly that as New Zealand was due to tour Pakistan shortly any number of Sutcliffe's pictures would appear many times in the press. He eventually went to Gordon College where he had access to a large number of cricket books from the college library. He found that many illustrations had been removed. He thought, 'what the heck', and did the same.

The London Book Depot was the largest bookshop in Rawalpindi, situated at the corner of its two premier roads. The Mani family owned it. They had a table full of cricket books laid down flat rather than being stacked in a bookshelf.

'Are you going to buy today?' the salesman would often ask me as I spent many an afternoon thumbing through them, drooling over every illustration.

'Not today,' I would usually reply although once a month I did buy a cricket magazine from them.

'Make sure you don't soil the books or I won't be able to sell them at all.' He was very indulgent as he must have known that I didn't have the wherewithal to buy any of them. Indeed, I'm not sure how many they sold. As late as 1958, the books on display were, *Farewell to Cricket* (Don Bradman, published 1950*), Playing for a Draw* (Trevor Bailey, 1953*), Express Deliveries* (Bill Bowes, reprinted 1954), *Bowling* (Alec Bedser, 1954), *The Ashes Crown the Year* (Jack Fingleton, 1954), *Test Status on Trial* (Hafeez Kardar, 1954), *Shabash Pakistan* (Sultan F Hussain, 1954), *Pakistan on the Cricket Map* (Qamaruddin Butt, 1954), *I Declare* (Jack Cheetham, 1955), *Just My Story (Len* Hutton*, 1956), Flying Stumps* (Ray Lindwall, paperback edition, 1958) and an instructional book by Alan Fairfax, an Australian cricketer, who toured England in 1930. How do I know all this? Well, I have a copy of each of them in my possession, apart from the Fairfax book, which I've never owned and the Bedser book, which I lent out in 1958 and never got back.

At the other end of the shop were all the comics, Dell and others. I was relatively late into comics. Indeed, I was relatively late into fiction. As late as thirteen or fourteen I was devouring the *Just William* books by Richmal Crompton. I progressed next to Conan Doyle and Agatha Christie, but I'm running too far ahead again.

Not content with reading books, late in 1956 I determined to write one. MCC were touring South Africa and I was determined to be the first out with a tour book. Speed was of the essence and I had a brainwave. Writing fresh copy would be time consuming, I would therefore produce a montage of press and cricket magazine reports. Copying from only one reporter would be plagiarism which would rightly be condemned.

However, if I copied from several sources and invested original thinking in determining what passages to include and what to leave out then, surely, it would constitute research? Armed with a scrapbook of such press cuttings of the first few matches, I went to a local stationer (I was too shy to go to the London Book Dept as too many people knew me). I had no idea that a stationer was not the same as a publisher. Anyway he sent me packing with a clip round my ear.

One day we had a cricket match on the school premises but after school. So I took my trainers, which we used to call PT shoes and were much more flimsy than the modern Nikes and Reboks, in a brown paper bag. We had our game and I went home in the evening. It was the following morning when I was getting ready for school that I realised that I'd come home in my trainers and left my shoes at the school ground. So I went to school in my trainers and went straight to the ground. The shoes had gone. I didn't have the courage to tell my father how I'd come to lose a fairly new pair of shoes. So I carried on like this for a couple of months. Then one day Dad threw a party for some friends of his and I had to put on my best clothes, which I did. But he noted that I wasn't wearing proper shoes. I said I would do in a minute. But eventually the secret came out. He asked me to go to my friend's place, in other words: to be scarce.

I did make myself scarce, but not the way he thought. Dad didn't smoke, but for the party he had bought several packets of cigarettes, Three Castles, Capstan, Gold Flake, etc. I nicked a couple of packets and, with my friend Javed Mahmood, went to our barn to smoke them. I lit a cigarette, inhaled, coughed and spluttered, tried again, inhaled, coughed and spluttered and so it went on until I'd worked my way through half a cigarette. By then I was in such a bad state that I lost all interest in smoking. I was eleven. I suspect that had I been a little older I might have got hooked.

The first first-class match I saw was in the winter of 1954/55 when India played the Combined Services XI. My father permitted me to go with our neighbours. We packed sandwiches. I can't remember what fluids we had. Bottled water was unknown and I was not then a tea drinker. It was a practically full house. The highlight for me was the batting of my hero, Imtiaz Ahmed. He was the top scorer in both innings (59 out of 105 all out, the only person to reach double figures, and 105 out of 183 all out). His lofted strokes are still in my memory but I have

Various pictures of my boyhood hero Imtiaz Ahmed

The sweep was a trademark stroke. Here he uses it against England at Lords and Nottingham, in 1954.

Against New Zealand in the 2nd Test in Lahore, 1955 Imtiaz hit 209 in a 307 run stand for the 7th wicket with Waqar Hasan. Three pictures, the first (previous page) shows him turn a ball to leg; the second reach his 100, the third a hook, a favourite shot, off Tony McGibbon The second and third pictures are on this page.

His other favourite stroke was the drive. Here are two examples of his cover drive executed in England in the ill-fated 1962 series.

Imtiaz was also a first-class wicket-keeper, safe but unshowy, like Keith
Andrew and Bob Taylor rather than Godfrey Evans.
Here he catches Hutton of Fazal at the Oval in 1954.
Hutton was out this way in both innings.

Here he stumps Graveney off Shuja, Manchester Test, 1954.

If only he had been a little more careful, his record would have been that much better; but, I daresay, we would have loved him less.
The Oval Test 1962 was his last. Top scorer in the first innings.
Top scorer in the second, on 98, against Larter with the new ball, he chases a wide one.

no recollection of his trademark sweep shot. Nor do I remember any of Lala Amarnath and Polly Umrigar's innings. I do however remember my other boyhood hero, Shujauddin, like me a mediocre right-hand batsman and left-arm spinner. He did nothing memorable but I saw him. Seeing both Imtiaz and Shuja – a Catholic seeing the Pope could not have been more overjoyed!

That series produced some turgid cricket, neither captain wanting to lose. However I had nothing to compare it with. I listened to radio commentary. Fazal Mahmood's bowling analysis of 25–18–19–0 in the first innings of the first Test convinced me that he was unplayable. After all the English couldn't play him, what chance the Indians? There was however another series being played, in Australia. Len Hutton was making the Aussies pay for past sufferings by unleashing Frank Tyson. The blood and thunder provided quite a contrast.

Next winter (1955/56) Donald Carr's MCC 'A' team arrived. It included one established Test player, Tony Lock and several highly promising players such as Ken Barringtom, Fred Titmus and Peter Richardson and other county stalwarts. Tony Lock, another left-arm spinner made an immediate impact. In the game before the first Test, he so mesmerised what was practically the Test batting line-up, that his first seventeen overs were maidens. Kardar broke the stranglehold by hitting him for four but perished in the same over. In the Peshawar 'Test' there was the infamous ragging incident. We boys didn't know what to make of it.

When they played a Combined Universities team, two of the players were Javed Burki and Ijaz Butt, who'd won school colours at St Mary's. They both played quite well, Butt narrowly missing a century.

The complaints about conduct on the field puzzled us. We had implicit belief in sportsmanship. The question of walking or not walking was not an issue. We assumed that all batsmen walked if they knew they'd nicked it. However there are degrees of excellence.

The supreme sportsman, than whom there was none better, was Imtiaz Ahmad. All of us boys believed in that, but I'm not sure where the idea came from in the first place.

Lock's success left a deep impression on me. Although Imtiaz Ahmed was my hero, my role models were Peter May as batsman and Tony Lock as bowler. I set myself a target of making the Pakistan team for the 1962 tour of England. Dad being an Anglophile, even then I had a deep affection for that country. Of course I'd only be seventeen in 1962 but talented Pakistanis emerge young. But I had to start by getting my contemporaries to take me seriously and that wasn't happening.

English cricket was reported daily in local newspapers, not just Test matches but also county matches. In 1956 we followed the Australian tour and were amazed at Jim Laker's achievements. We were even more astonished at how little success Lock had in the same matches. None of us had seen either of them, but we believed that Lock was the better bowler and Laker's success was a fluke.

In the mid-fifties a monthly magazine called *Sportimes* started appearing. About half of it was devoted to cricket, the rest to other sport. It covered, with occasional articles, American sports such as baseball and basketball but I can't recall a single article on football. So I knew all about Roger Maris and Mickey Mantle but nothing about Ferenc Puskas, Stanley Matthews and Billy Wright. It gave extensive coverage to the Melbourne Olympics of 1956. I knew all about the achievements of Bob Morrow/Betty Cuthbert/Al Oerter/Vladimir Kutz and Charlie Dumas. I knew of the love affair of Hal Connolly of the US and Olga Fikotova of Hungary. Of course I became interested in track and field events. There were two grounds within a mile of my house. One was the cricket ground belonging to the Rawalpindi Club, where I saw India play Combined Services. Across the road from it was an athletics stadium. They were readying it for some event and my friend Javed and I used it for about a month. We raced round the track and tried high and long jumps. I got beaten every time but it did not worry me.

One day I went on my own and had a go at all the events. There was a bearded man there wearing the Pakistani dress of shalwar/kameez with a waistcoat as it was cold. He started watching me, encouraging me, in the high jump to jump with both feet instead of trying to straddle it as I was doing. He then asked me to rest and sat down next to me and said words of encouragement. He could see real talent in me. He then put his hand on mine. I did not know how to react. He then lifted my hand and placed it on his prick. I winced and yanked my hand free and fled. He did not chase me.

A week or so later I went to Javed's house to see if he wanted to play cricket that evening. His Mum said he was receiving Qu'ran lessons but would be free shortly. She asked me to wait in the lounge but not to disturb him. So in I went. Who did I see there teaching Javed the

Qu'ran? The pervert from the athletics stadium! There was a look of fear on his face. He was wondering what I would say. But what could I say? Who'd believe me?

Late in March, Javed came to my place on his bike, handed me an envelope and disappeared. He was careful to avoid eye contact with either me or Mum who happened to be about. It was an invitation to a party in a few days. Mum looked at it and worked out that the date was the first of April. (Incidentally that was the day in Tunbridge Wells when a Mrs Gower gave birth to a son, David Ivor.) She said immediately, 'It is an April Fool's joke.' I sensed that she must be right, as Javed was trying his best not to giggle. However I determined to go with my eyes open. 'Nobody can catch me out.'

When I got there I realised that it was an exclusive party. There were only three people, Javed, me and his elder sister. She must have been in her late teens and she sat at the head of the table and cajoled me into eating everything. I was so mesmerised – or rather overawed – that I did as I was told. First came samosas and pakoras (a.k.a. onion bhaajis). Then she took a slab and cut a thick slice and gave it to me. I did not recognise it as anything edible so she reassured me,

'It is cheese, cheddar cheese. English people eat it.'

Cheese is not unknown in Pakistan but it was unknown to me. But this bar looked more like Sunlight soap but her instructions were firm.

So, obediently I took a bite and was about to spit it out when she told me off for having bad eating habits. So I swallowed it, called it quits and fled. All the time Javed was in stitches.

In 1957/58 Pakistan toured the West Indies for the first time. Because of the time difference, newspaper reports were way too late and we had to rely on radio news for updates. It was a high-scoring series with two triple centuries, one each by Hanif Mohammed and Garry Sobers. We didn't know it at the time, but Hanif had so lost his poise against Roy Gilchrist that he daren't open. We knew that he'd dropped down to number four by the third Test as it was there in the scorecard, but we didn't know why until Kardar's tour book was published a couple of years later. Imtiaz was the batsman who stood up to and caned Gilchrist.

The year 1958 was the first year I was in a class taught by Mr Rogers. A big man, it was impossible to guess his age but seeing as his mother, with whom he lived, was very sprightly, was probably in his mid-thirties. He had a stern manner but was quite gentle; and an excellent teacher.

He and his mother were that rare breed, the English who stayed behind after independence. He was born in Rawalpindi and regarded England as an alien land. Years later, I heard that a time came in the late sixties or early seventies, when he felt that Pakistan was changing and there was no future there for him. So he migrated to England only to find that if he was not Pakistani, he was English even less; one of the many unnoticed casualties of history. A bigger casualty was the sizeable Christian community, who suffered because some of them had sided with the British in the past. This was unfair discrimination. Most of these Christians were from the poorer part of society whom the Christian missionaries had converted and provided with food and succour.

Rawalpindi was an American base and the American influence was strong. They probably spied on the Russians. Gary Powers, whose U2 plane was shot down over USSR in 1960, took off from Peshawar, a city near Rawalpindi. There were three Americans in my class in 1958, big fleshy blokes, always in jeans. There was regular banter between them and Mr Rogers.

My idyllic life suffered dislocation when Dad was sent to Los Angeles on a six-month management development programme. He sent his family to Kerala so that we could meet our relatives after a six-year gap. I was there when West Indies played a five Test series and slaughtered an Indian team riven by factions. Sobers was in great form and Kanhai at last came good. However it was the fast bowling of Gilchrist and Hall that was the deciding factor. I was still in Kerala when they moved to Pakistan to play three Tests. Roy Gilchrist had been sent home for persisting in bowling beamers. That undoubtedly weakened them, although Hall was in great form. Pakistan won the first two Tests and lost the third. The second Test, which was won by Fazal's bowling, would have been lost but for stands between Wallis Mathias and Shujauddin in both innings. In the third Test, Kanhai got a double century and Pakistan opened with Imtiaz and Ijaz Butt, the latter being the owner of St Mary's School colours and the current head of the Pakistan Cricket Board. Butt stopped a Hall delivery with his mouth and went off injured. Imtiaz launched a furious attack on Hall but he was out for 41 and Hall later took a hat trick. Mushtaq Mohammed made his debut in this Test, becoming the youngest Test player ever.

However this series was small beer. The main fare was an Ashes series with Peter May leading out a team that was billed as the strongest to leave English shores. The reason for the confidence was partly because it was felt that Australia was weak. Benaud and Davidson had carried the attack the previous winter against South Africa but Peter May couldn't see how they could have improved from the relatively innocuous bowlers they were in 1956. How wrong he was! Both had become world-class bowlers.

However, what made the wheels come off was that Australia had a whole collection of chuckers and draggers, Meckiff, Rorke, Burke and Slater. England made a mistake in not complaining at the very start. Once Meckiff had bowled them out for 87 at Melbourne it would have sounded like whingeing. Mind you, having turned a blind eye to Tony Lock, England were hardly in a position to complain.

They lost the series 4–1.

I was heartbroken when, on his return from the US, Dad was transferred to Lahore. There I joined St Anthony's, another missionary school on par with St Mary's. Although I didn't know it, Majid Khan, whom I came to idolise ten years later when he played for Pakistan, was at the same school, a year younger than me.

Before the year was out, Dad got transferred again, this time to Karachi. New friends, a new environment and puberty all contributed to a metamorphosis. Gone was the gregarious individual who blurted out anything that came to mind without filtering it through a sieve of tact, replaced by someone who became reluctant to say much, particularly in female company.

I joined St Patrick's, another Catholic missionary school, but they were a mixture of Brothers and Fathers, rather than just Fathers. Fathers are senior to Brothers. In convent schools they have not just Sisters and Mothers but also a Mother Superior. All the Brothers and Fathers at St Patrick's were of Goan extraction. It was a good school but not in the same league as St Mary's or St Anthony's. I did my 'O' levels in 1960.

Karachi was quite different to Rawalpindi. The climate was not as nice, very humid, where Rawalpindi was dry. It also didn't get cold in the winter. It was a much more cosmopolitan city. There were plenty of foreign nationals. Also most of the people who migrated to Pakistan after partition settled in or around Karachi. Around about this time, the political capital was moved to a newly created city called Islamabad, next door to the army headquarters. Karachi remained the commercial capital.

By now there were murmurs of missionary schools corrupting the youth of the country. So the Lord's prayer was withdrawn and replaced by hymns that made no reference to the Holy Trinity and could therefore be regarded as universal, hymns such as *All things bright and beautiful*. Out went the history book written by Rev. Marsden, which depicted Robert Clive and Warren Hastings as heroes and Muhammad Bin Tughlak, the king who moved the capital from Delhi to a brand-new city, Fatehpur Sikri, only to find that it had no water, as an eccentric buffoon. In came a textbook produced by the Ministry of Education and, suddenly, Clive and Hastings were villains and Muhammad Bin Tughlak a misunderstood genius. The Ministry of Education had one problem: what title to give the book? It is extremely difficult to write the history of Pakistan without writing the history of India; its like writing about Eve without Adam or the history of Wales without mentioning England. So they called it the *History of Hind-Pakistan*.

Although cricket was played seriously at the school (it had its own ground and, in Jacob Harris, a former first class cricketer as a coach and famous Test players such as Wallis Mathias and India's Ramchand as alumni) I did not play cricket.

In the winter of 1960/61 were played two contrasting series. In India, Pakistan took part in a series of unremitting boredom. It was generally the fifth day before both sides completed their first innings. The thought of losing to its neighbour was unthinkable to both sides. Home team bias was obvious in umpiring, as indeed it was when India toured Pakistan in 1954/5.

Meanwhile Australia and the West Indies were taking part in the most exciting series since 1902. Worrell's team played aggressive cricket from the start and Benaud replied in kind. Three of the five matches went to the wire.

In 1961 I joined Karachi Grammar School in the sixth form to do my A levels; an outstanding school, with a proper balance between education and sport. It took cricket seriously but had no record of producing first class cricketers. I took up cricket again, but alas I wasn't good enough to make my house second team and they didn't have a third. I still followed the game avidly but I reconciled myself to the role of a fan.

I saw one day of the Karachi Test against England and saw Ted Dexter score a marvellous 205 and Mike Smith 56. Parfitt came in late in the day and went on to score a century the following day; the first of many that year, as he gorged himself against weak bowling. I remember

Mike Smith, his face ruddy, his shirt billowing in the Karachi breeze. I also remember Ted Dexter skipping down the pitch to the spinners. The great Fazal Mahmood, heavier than in the Oval Test photographs, was fiendishly accurate still, but lacking in penetration. But the other memories were beyond the boundary. I went with a friend of mine. At the turnstile next to ours there was a queue of perhaps ten young men. One-by-one they filed in saying that the last one would pay for the tickets, but when it came to the supposed last man, he said he was nothing to do with them. Also, there was a students' enclosure with cheap seats. My mate and I were surprised how many mature students there were.

The last game I watched in Karachi was one organised for a charitable cause. Two teams of current and former Test players played a one-innings match at the Karachi Parsi Institute. I went along the previous day to see the players practising. Kardar was there as were Hanif, Imtiaz and Fazal and a limping Nazar Mohammad. A key batsman for Pakistan in the early fifties, Nazar was having an amorous tryst with Noor Jehan, Pakistan's Marilyn Monroe, when her husband turned up. Nazar jumped out of the bedroom window and broke his leg, ending his cricket career.

The match itself was a bit boring, Imtiaz, conscious that the crowd wanted entertainment scored an attractive half century but Hanif batting down the order sent us to sleep. When the match was over, players disappeared quicker than it would take an umpire to say 'Stumps'; all the players except Imtiaz. He had his clothes in a canvas bag and changed out of his cricket gear in the outfield shielded by a large group of fans, I among them. It was strange to see your childhood hero, a colossus in your imagination and find that he was a mere 5 feet 8 or at best 9. He didn't say anything but smiled a shy smile as he changed. He did not wear pants, so I was able to confirm what I guess I knew anyway given the way he took on Tyson, Hall and Gilchrist, Imtiaz had balls.

In 1962 Pakistan's cricket team hit a low point on its second visit to England. This was the tour I was targeting to go on, a long-abandoned ambition. The performance was the antithesis of what the team had stood for. There was no spine, no pride no resistance. They had to thank the Manchester weather for avoiding a 5–0 whitewash. They started off on the wrong foot when Javed Burki, the same one who won school colours at St Mary's, was named captain. Team unity didn't exist and the bowling was weak. Haseeb Ahsan was sent home for an allegedly suspect action. The only two to emerge with credit were Imtiaz Ahmed and the young Mushtaq Mohammed.

There was some unintended humour. The team manager, Brigadier Hyder, knew nothing about cricket. During one Test, Alimuddin had hit two dogged fifties in a lost cause. He was on the massage table having a rub down when the brigadier saw him.

'What is this, Alim, your country needs you and you're relaxing?'

'But I've batted already brigadier.'

'Never mind, your country needs you. Go out and bat again.'

In December 1962 I took my A levels and had a few months' grace before starting college in September. In January I therefore took two months' holiday to visit Kerala in India, where my parents hailed from and where my paternal grandparents and cousins and uncles still lived. There I met Kadeeja. I'm not sure what she saw in me but we struck up a rapport and maintained contact by correspondence after I returned

Kadeeja, a youthful vision.

30

from holiday. She went on to do great things at college and eventually in 1970 we got married.

There was no career guidance in those days. In Karachi Grammar School a pattern emerged. If you were good in maths, you went for engineering; if you were good in biology, you went for medicine; if you were good at neither but could handle arithmetic, you studied accountancy; if you were good at nothing, you joined the army. There was another group of students who were from the mercantile class, mainly people who had migrated from Gujarat and Maharashtra in India. They were the goldsmiths, the moneylenders and the traders. In the main, their children were pulled back into the family firm without tertiary education.

So I was set on a career in engineering, chemical engineering. I could have studied in Karachi University but I wanted to go abroad. I checked out the cost and found that it would have cost my father his entire salary to support me. But he did not flinch, saying that he would borrow from his pension fund. The debt I owe him is immeasurable. I applied for a Shell scholarship (to study in Loughborough College) but did not get it. I managed to get a place in Loughborough though. I also applied and got a place in MIT in Massachusetts, *the* place for engineering but even more expensive.

In the event I didn't go. Deep down I knew that I wasn't an engineer and the thought of crippling my father bothered me. Late in the day I heard of an actuarial career and after some investigation I opted for it. Not only was the subject to my liking, you studied while you worked, freeing my father from having to support me.

In order to be accepted as an actuarial student, you had to sit an entrance exam, which was completely maths based. Before you could do that, your application had to be sponsored by two actuaries. There were only four actuaries in Pakistan and I approached two of them. One was the local General Manager for Norwich Union and the other, Sami Hasan, barely twenty-three but mature beyond his years, had recently returned from England to become the Actuary of Habib Insurance. Luckily both agreed to sponsor me.

In November 1963 I sat the entrance exam and had the shock of my life. Having been accustomed to getting perhaps half a question wrong in maths exams, I thought I'd be lucky to get 40%. I might have been the last person who scraped over the line but somehow I passed. I then took and passed the first two subjects in Karachi

I had wasted a year trying to make my mind up. In the process I missed seeing Worrell's team who toured England in 1963. I never saw him bat but by all accounts his stroke play was exquisite. The Lord's Test was particularly exciting.

I worked for six months in Habib Insurance. It was routine clerical work but Sami saw enough of me to satisfy himself that I would make the grade. He gave me a letter of introduction to Northern Insurance Company, for whom he had worked when training as an actuary.

One Saturday, when I left the office late, I was going to take an auto-rickshaw to get me home quickly as I was hungry. The office was quite near the terminus of trams. Trams were quite common in Karachi although they operated on a limited number of routes. One of these went close to my house. As I was about to hail an auto-rickshaw I saw a tram head towards the terminus. I made a snap decision to catch it, and catch it before it got to the terminus, so as to avoid having to queue. I swung round and caught the handrail hoping to board it. As I did that from a stationary position and the tram was travelling, it dragged me. I had to let go and fell down. My left forefinger came under the wheel and the minced portion had to be amputated. This happened a month before I was due to leave for England.

The day before I left for England, we went for a group photograph of the family. Later that evening, a close family friend of ours came with his family to bid me good bye. He warned me that, 'There are three traps that young men must avoid; wine, women and gambling.' It was a strange thing to say but I suspect that Dad must have asked him to give me some advice. He had kitted me out for the English weather. Through someone he had purchased for me a trilby and a raincoat and he insisted that I wore both when I boarded the aircraft. Inside my trousers I was wearing long-johns ('It's cold in London', Dad insisted.) My finger had not fully healed and was heavily bandaged. All in all, I was quite a sight when I landed at Heathrow, London on 10th October 1964.

2. 1965

As the plane circled prior to landing in the afternoon, I was surprised at the drabness of houses; all red-tiled and neat but small. After going through customs I boarded the coach which took me to the Victoria terminus. My best friend from Karachi Grammar School, Naseem, was there to meet me. His family had settled in London and I was to board with them. He came with a friend, the expression on whose face upon seeing me suggested that he was thinking, 'Bloody hell, what have we got here?' I discarded the trilby the following day and the raincoat, which I discovered was what schoolboys wore, not long after. Dad had also tried to buy me a sports jacket but didn't manage it, so he insisted that I took his. It was far too large for a skinny nineteen-year-old and I discarded that too. As I was only allowed 20kg of luggage, I'd left my entire collection of cricket pictures and press cuttings, save one album which I brought with me.

Naseem's family lived in a large detached house in Cricklewood, north-west London. It was a Victorian or Edwardian house. They let out upstairs although Naseem lived upstairs too. He and I shared a large room. We slept in bunk-beds. There was one wardrobe between us and one study desk and one dressing table and one settee, which luckily could seat two. Heating was by pink paraffin heaters which had to be put out at night. This was done in the landing as it emitted unpleasant fumes. Naseem was an accountancy student who never studied, so we never fought over the use of the desk.

Britain was in the midst of a general election. I arrived on the 10th, polling day being the 16th October. Democracy was new to me and it was fascinating to watch the two main parties slugging it out. It was like watching a boxing contest. Each side was determined to knock the other out, asked for no quarter and gave none. And yet there were unarticulated rules that they obeyed. Harold Wilson was ubiquitous.

With his dry voice and purposeful mannerm he seemed a modern man and provided a striking contrast to Alec Douglas Home who was all decorum and, it seemed, not much more. Labour won by the narrowest of margins and I was amazed at how easy the transfer of power was; no skulduggery. I did not know then that Alec Home was a cricketer who had played for Eton in his time.

Cricklewood and neighbouring Kilburn were largely white but included a large Irish community. Mike Gatting must have lived nearby because he went to our local school, John Kelly's Boys School. John Embury lived in Willesden, which was a mile away and had a strong West Indian community. All three areas were to have a large Asian influx over the next six years.

I had with me a letter of recommendation which enabled me to get a job as an actuarial student at the Northern Insurance Company. The Head Office was in several buildings within half a mile of Bank station in the City of London. I was to work in a rectangular concrete-and-glass building at 29 Gresham Street. I started on the twenty-sixth of the same month I arrived in London on a salary of £535 p.a. with three half-days a week for study during the winter months. Holidays were only two weeks a year, but we had free lunch. The office hours were 9am to 4.45pm. An attendance book was kept at the ground floor reception and we had to sign in on arrival. At 9am a blue line was drawn to see who were late. At 9.05 a red line was drawn and the attendance book taken to the office of a formidable-looking manager and we had to sign in his presence. Everyone wore a sober suit and tie with a plain white or light blue or cream shirt. Some of the senior staff wore bowlers.

For lunch we had to go to the plebs' canteen in Basinghall Street, some two hundred yards away. Lunch was of good quality. We had three courses, soup being the starter. One day a week we had omelette, another day steak, one day fish and chips, another day, liver and bacon. Some days we had egg curry, but other than that, it was English food all the way. One day they served faggots and not knowing what it was, I asked and was told, 'Its like curry, you don't ask what's in it; you just eat it.' Whatever I ate, I had chips and peas with it. Mushrooms were a new and pleasurable experience but I can't recall seeing broccoli or parsnips. My preferred dessert was ice cream. Strawberry and chocolate flavours were a new experience but other flavours such as pistachio had not yet reached these shores.

Between 9.15 and 9.30 a tea lady would come with tea, which was free, and spam rolls and such like for which we paid. Plebs like me poured tea out of a tap into paper cups. Section leaders got tea served in china cups and superintendents were served in their own pots delivered on a tray.

My starting salary after tax gave me a take home pay of £36/month. I paid £21/month for board and lodging. My monthly season ticket, on the underground, cost £3.12s.6d (i.e. £3.625). That left around £11/month for clothes, entertainment, etc. What saved me was that Dad had arranged for me to have £150 to cover me for three months in case I had trouble finding a job. As I found one inside a month, I had £100 to spare. I bought myself two suits from Horne Bros and a coat from John Collier. I can't recall where the balance went.

The Actuarial Department was headed by Brian Dawson who was a superintendent. He had his own cubicle with five-foot-high translucent glass on three sides. My boss Dave Reynolds was a section leader who reported to Brian. He had a team of junior and more experienced students working for him. I started as the only junior who had to do all the work whilst others, such as Colin Coles, were the 'checkers.' Our job was to provide non-standard quotations. So we were in constant touch with our branches. Northern didn't deal direct with clients but via brokers. We had salesmen, called 'Inspectors' whose job it was to persuade brokers to give us business. Many of these Inspectors were glorified post collectors. They all wore bowler hats.

Colin Coles took charge of me and showed me how to do one set of calculation. He then said, 'Right, you must now draft a letter.' He took a prototype letter and said, 'Come with me.' We walked across the length of the building until we reached a room at the other end marked 'Dictation Room'. He gave me a folder which contained a disc the size of an LP but floppy. He sat in front of a machine and put the disc on it and switched it on.

'Right, this is a dictation machine. You speak into it the contents of the letter you want typed. But first you must erase what's already on it.' He then did just that and dictated into it. He prefaced it with the comment, 'Hello, Jean we've got a new junior by the name of Iqbal. I'm showing him how to use this machine.'

We then went two floors down to a large room marked 'Typing Pool' with a female population. At the far end sat a formidable-looking lady called Jean Sharman. She looked me up and down and with a brief smile said, 'Hello.' She then added,

'If you want something done quickly, mark it urgent,' then, after a pause, and in a louder voice, 'If you start marking everything urgent, we'll ignore the instructions.'

I went back suitably warned. The checkers must have done other things too, as doing is harder than checking. Arithmetic was never my strong suit and I would often make mistakes. The calculation would be thrown back at me without any indication of where the error was so I had to go through the entire calculation again. I was the junior until Allen Kelly arrived eighteen months later. It's Allen, not Alan, I'm told the mistake was made by the Registrar.

One day I made a mistake in the letter I had drafted and had to take it down to the typing pool to Jean.

'You want the letter retyped do you?'

'Yes, please.'

'Did one of my girls make the mistake?'

'No.'

'Then who did?'

'I did.'

'You made the mistake and we have to put it right?'

'Er, yes.'

'Is it a complete retype?'

'No, some of the numbers are wrong.'

'Do you realise how hard it is to correct the original and the two carbons?'

'Yes, I mean no.'

'Don't do it again.'

But I was never perfect. I continued to make mistakes much to Jean's annoyance. I was more scared of her than of my boss Dave. In due course I was to discover that she had a heart of gold; that everyone made mistakes and it was my meekness that Jean mocked.

Having studied in English-medium schools I was not expecting any language problems, but there were differences. I remember when someone at work asked me if I fancied a game of tennis. I said I didn't have a racket. No problem, he had a spare one. I said I had no knickers. He burst out laughing saying, 'What do you want knickers for?' I should have said shorts. On another occasion I went to British Home Stores to buy briefs but didn't know what they were called. I asked a girl, 'Where can I find men's underclothing?', 'Men under what?' she asked. At school we'd picked up a lot of American slang from films. Thus 'bucks' or 'chips' were used where in England we use 'quid' and, of course, I didn't know what half-a-crown or a tanner were. As for rhyming slang, I'd heard nothing like it.

At work I drafted a letter to a prospective client containing the sentence, 'I enclose a form for completion at your convenience,' only to be told obliquely 'No he'll use a toilet roll for that.' I just did not get it until someone told me that toilets were called conveniences.

There was a fair amount of what we'd now call 'racist' banter at work from a couple of people, but it didn't worry me. I'd been used to sledging at school, what with being darker-skinned than the average Pakistani and short. None of them worried me. The taunts at work were of the type, 'What did you learn at school, Iqbal? I know Notting Hill 3/6d, Ladbroke Grove two shillings; mind the doors.' One day I was asked to read out the Siamese National Anthem and shown a piece of paper with the words

Oh watan a Siam

If you say it fast enough, it should come out as *Oh, what an ass I am*. What they didn't know was that 'wathan' in Urdu means country so I assumed that it must mean the same in Siamese and read the words as *Oh wathan-e-Siam*, an altogether different sound. Rather like sledging in the cricket field, it ceased pretty quickly as people realised that I wasn't bothered by it.

Generally, there were misconceptions on both sides. The great economic migration of the fifties, which had been clamped down by the time I arrived, was actively sought by London Transport, the National Health Service and the cotton mills of Lancashire. In the main, these immigrants were semi-literate people who spoke little or no English and therefore preferred to stick to their own rather than mix with the natives. The second wave was of people who would service this expatriate community; the butchers, restauranteurs, etc. And there were a relatively few like me who came for tertiary education. My overriding impression of the English, when I first arrived, was that they all looked alike: pink.

The English thought that the Asian shift-workers were filthy; that they shared a bed (not simultaneously) and even shoes. The Asians thought the English were filthy because they bathed weekly not daily.

Both could find examples in support of their belief but were wrong to extrapolate that to the entire community.

I normally lunched with Kevin and a few colleagues from other sections, my section being small we had to take turns to make sure that someone was always there to take phone calls. One of the guys I lunched with worked in the Claims Department. One day he came to me with a policy document. Somebody who had died had a policy that covered the outstanding mortgage on death. As the mortgage will gradually reduce over the years, the sum assured would depend upon when he died. So the policy had a table of percentages. You simply multiplied the original sum insured, i.e. the initial mortgage amount by the percentage appropriate to the year in which he died.

So he came to me and said, pointing to the document, 'Iqbal, what is 95% of £1,000?'

I looked at him as I felt sure that he was winding me up. But he seemed genuine enough. I thought to myself, 'Gosh, this guy's a thicko', and told him the answer. Some months later we were strolling after lunch when he popped into the bookies and I followed him. He collected winnings on a four to five on and placed half-a-crown on some other complex accumulator and he seemed to know exactly how much he could win. I couldn't even begin to define the problem, never mind calculate the result.

In the early years I passed exams quite regularly (ten subjects to pass in all) and, although I don't remember precisely, my salary was probably pushing £700 p.a. by the end of 1965.

Until then, entertainment comprised trips to Hyde Park or the West End, the journey being covered by the rail season ticket, or seeing the occasional film. When I first came to England the posters were for *Behold a Pale Horse* (Gregory Peck and Anthony Quinn), *The Servant* (Dirk Bogarde and Sarah Miles), *The Agony and the Ecstasy* (Charlton Heston), *Arabesque* (Gregory Peck and Sophia Loren), *Yesterday Today and Tomorrow* (Sophia Loren and Marcello Mastroianni), *Zorba the Greek* (Anthony Quinn and Alan Bates) and *Roustabout* (Elvis Presley). Sunday Night at the London Palladium was compèred not by Bruce Forsyth but by Norman Vaughan. *Danger Man* and *The Saint* were the other compulsory viewings on the television. Also on television were two cricketers appearing in commercials. Ted Dexter promoted Noilly Prat whilst Fred Trueman promoted De Beer diamonds ('I'm only here for De Beer', he says in a pub). Fred also appeared in some television programmes. The one I remember is the Dickie Henderson Show where he agreed to turn out in a cricket match.

I remember being bowled over by Roy Orbison singing *Pretty Woman*, still my all-time favourite pop song, at the London Palladium. On another occasion the Beatles sang *Eight Days a Week* and their latest No. 1, *I Feel Fine*.

The film that made a stunning impression on me was *Goldfinger*, the first Bond film that I saw and still, in my opinion, the best. Sean Connery was superb and I found the tension unbearable, particularly in the scene where he was going to be carved up by a laser beam. Another film I thoroughly enjoyed was Peter Sellers's *A Shot in the Dark*. It was the second Pink Panther film.

In music I was a Beatles fan and didn't care for the Stones. I also came to like Western classical music, having my initiation via Rimsky Korsakoff's Scheherezade, Strauss's Blue Danube and Beethoven's Fifth Symphony. I was a regular visitor to two record stores; the HMV in Oxford Street near Bond Street Station (sited on the opposite side of the road to the present shop) and Imhofs in Tottenham Court Road. Both of them allowed you to listen at length to LPs and you could get an hour's entertainment at no cost.

Not far from the Imhof shop, practically next door to the British Museum, was the YMCA. Naseem and I joined it. There was no entrance fee and although the C in the name stood for Christian, there was no preaching, simply an exhortation at the time we joined to 'read about it'. Most members were foreigners and we could play table tennis there. A trip to the record shop followed by a game of table tennis and a glass of squash made for a perfect Saturday afternoon.

We worked hard but we also had a lot of fun. Modern managers would not tolerate the extent to which we wasted time. But it wasn't just us kids who were inefficient. Looking back, there were quite a few people marooned in middle-management who, these days, would have been got rid of. One was a New Zealand actuary; another, the actuary in charge of Valuation who was unable to control his staff (I give an example later). Another was someone who didn't complete his exams and looked after the actuarial aspects of Northern's dwindling African business.

The late Peter Clark, who worked for the great Prudential once told me that, in the late seventies when he was promoted to Superintendent, his first step on the managerial ladder, his terms of employment changed. Instead of working 9 to 5, his working hours were reduced to 9.30 to 4.30. By then, there was greater pressure from competitors for business and, in practice, Peter worked long hours. But, he said to me, there were several older Superintendents who worked only from 9.30 to 4.30. I suppose it was ever thus; those who were ambitious worked long hours but others were content to coast. I wasn't aware of similar discrepancy in Northern's working hours but we certainly had separate dining rooms though not as many as at the Pru which had eight.

Anyway, back to the Northern of 1965, here are a few examples of pranks. One day I went to the bank to draw £5 out in cash. In the adjacent queue was a colleague who was drawing ten pounds. The girl at the till looked sideways at a list, presumably to check if he was on some sort of black list. He clearly wasn't as she took the money out, and handed out the crisp pound notes:

'Here you are Sir, 1, 2, 3, 4, 5, 6, 7, 8, 9, 10.'

My colleague took the money, and counted, '1, 2, 3, 4, 5, 6, 7, 8, 9, 10, 11, 12'

'Is everything all right Sir?' she asked.

'Yes, thank you,' he said saluting her and quickly leaving the branch.

The poor girl was frantic as she counted how many notes were remaining in the wad from which she had taken them out. I'm sure she was OK.

There was another young guy who was prematurely bald and nobody important at that stage in his life, a junior clerk like me. However, he wore a pin stripe suit, white shirt with detachable collars and cufflinks and a sober tie. When he emerged in the morning from the Bank tube station, a bowler on his head and a Telegraph and an umbrella in his armpit, he had a gravitas that commanded attention. He looked every inch a stockbroker. And yet he was an outrageous prankster and would do unbelievable stunts with a complete poker face. He liked nothing better than to embarrass people in public, but was the soul of decorum at work. He once confronted me in Cheapside saying,

'Where's my £25?'

'What £25?' I asked.

'Ah, you've forgotten it already have you?' he asked, raising his voice slightly.

'I don't owe you anything.'

'Typical,' he said raising his voice further. 'It's typical of you people. You come into this country without any money. I bail you out and what do you do by way of reward? You try to get out of it.'

A small crowd of people who pretended not to be listening was gathering and I was beginning to get worried. How do you prove that you haven't borrowed money? Then suddenly he hugged me and said, 'I forgive you, you can give it to me next month.'

What was I to do next? Leave it at that and let people have a low opinion of me? Or continue to challenge him and be made to look even more ungrateful?

I chose the former; not because I was a coward, but because I was no match for his capacity to put on a show. Some months later I tried to gain revenge. After a few days reconnoitring, I confronted him as he came out of Bank station.

'Ah, there you are, the police are waiting for you. You'd better come with me.'

He ignored me.

'Did you hear me? You've been rumbled. You sold shares you didn't own. The City of London police are after you.'

He put on an air of such innocence that everyone started looking at me as if I was the criminal rather than the apprehender. To compound matters, I burst out laughing.

There were other occasions when I was the perpetrator not the butt of leg-pulls. Two celebrity clients of ours were Reggie Maudling, the outgoing Chancellor of the Exchequer and the Baroness Burton of Coventry. Colin Coles had dealt with both of them. I wrote a letter, ostensibly from the former, complaining about our service and said that the latter had a similar complaint. It was a gentle leg-pull at Colin's expense and I thought he'd see through it. He didn't and he dutifully reported the complaint to Brian Dawson and before I knew it, it had escalated to the Actuary of the company. I'm not sure where I obtained access to a typewriter but the letter clearly sounded authentic. In the end I had to come clean and suffer a dressing down.

There was one Inspector who had an office in the Shell Centre at Waterloo. All he did was to be at the beck and call of Shell employees. Once he phoned Actuarial to chase some piece of work and I answered the call. A combination of my high-pitched voice and my accent convinced him that I was a Scots lass and being a Scotsman himself, proceeded to chat me up. I didn't know whether to be flattered or offended. He turned up one afternoon and his disappointment on seeing me was visible to all.

Adjacent to the Actuarial Department was the Valuation Department and there were two guys there who spent a major part of the day playing chess. Each of them had a pocket chess set in his drawer. They'd make a move and hand it on a scrap of paper and the other guy would open his drawer make the move on his chess board, mull it over and send his response. Work would pile up, so they did paid overtime. Their boss knew about this but was not firm enough to deal with it.

I could fill a whole book of pranks people at the Northern got up to, but as they didn't involve me they have no place in this book. As is the way of the world, they targeted the touchy or the meek. One Nigerian who wanted to be an actuarial student but couldn't make it was a particular target.

One thing I had to get used to very quickly was protocol. The Actuary of the Life Department was a Ken Le Cras. He could only be addressed by us as Mr Le Cras. That was fair enough. But if he wanted to talk to Colin Coles who was just a student or even Dave Reynolds, a qualified actuary on the first rung of the managerial ladder, he'd call them by their surname: 'Coles, can you come here' or 'Have you got a minute, Reynolds.' Sometimes he'd pop out of his office and ask,

'Anyone going to the shops?'

We'd all keep our heads down and one guy, a toady, would stand up and say,

'I'm going,' or sometimes, 'I'll go.'

When they started calling you by your Christian name, you have arrived. This was a problem for me. I have no surname. My father isn't an Iqbal. He and Mum call me Iqbal so I wasn't in the least bit offended when everyone in the Northern called me Iqbal. But I minded being called Muhammad. It is a name often given but seldom used as it is the Prophet's name. It's a bit like if you're called Christian Fletcher, you wouldn't like your first name shortened would you? Somewhere along the line I picked up the nickname Icki and I grabbed it with both hands. At least it's better than my nickname in Karachi Grammar School, which was Hitler – taken from the words to the Col Bogey March, *Ik* in

Punjabi means *one,* so Iqbal became *one-ball.*

Northern had a wide variety of social and sporting activities. I joined the Chess Club. I had never played the game but in 1963, after leaving school, I'd bought myself a book on how to play it. That's not the same thing as playing it, of course, and I was roundly thrashed, once being Fools Mated. I quickly found my own level, which was in the fourth team. There were some serious players in the first two teams.

Naseem's family were Shia Muslims (although his mother was a Catholic) whilst I came from Sunni stock. Shias and Sunnis are not supposed to get on. Nothing could be further from the truth. We got on famously, even though I wasn't religious, whereas, in his middle age Naseem's father had become quite religious. He used to hold several *majlis* where a cleric recites the story of the last days of the Prophet's grandson who was slaughtered by his political enemies. I attended some of these sessions but found the sight of old men weeping funny. It was quite difficult to repress a smile.

Like all Muslims I avoided pork although I was partial to Scotch eggs. I was teetotal but that was no disadvantage as I simply avoided pubs in my first two years.

Naseem's parents and sister Zeenat on her birthday, 22.2.1965.
Standing left to right are (friend) Ali, Naseem and myself

A bigger problem was that I was a non-smoker and, therefore, out of step with the majority. I found the smoke in cinema halls irritating. I did briefly try to take up smoking but did not take to it.

During the month of *Ramzan* Muslims are supposed to fast from dawn to dusk, no solids or liquids or even gas, i.e. no smoking. Naseem's father used to fast. I did the same during weekends as there would be no food in the house. In my first year, during the week, I used to go to work without breakfast, as if I was fasting but had lunch in the canteen but I did not eat a full meal as I had to look hungry when it was time to break the fast in the evening. I dispensed with the pretence after the first year. *Ramzan* was followed by the *Eid-ul-Fitr*. We went to the Regent's Park Mosque for prayers. One of our group was a dandy and always wore expensive shoes polished to shine like patent leather. It is customary to take off one's shoes before saying one's prayers. When he returned after the prayers, he found that his shoes had been stolen. (I was safe as my shoes were scruffy and of small size). After an initial panicky look around, he stole the next best pair around and left hastily.

Test cricket was being played during the winter but far away. England toured South Africa. Mike Smith was captain and Fred Trueman, who'd missed the 1956/57 tour, the one on which I was going to write a tour book, because he was not a good diplomat, missed this one as he was deemed to be past his best. That was probably true, but surely he was better than some of those chosen in his stead? Cartwright and Thomson, typical English-conditions bowlers, and David Brown and John Price. Cartwright apart, do you remember any of them? Perhaps you may remember John Price. He had an unbelievable run up. It started at mid-off where he stood facing the sight screen. If you imagine an upside down J with a long upright stem he would run along the curvy handle and smoothly reverse direction. He had toured India in 1963/4 under Mike Smith, a tour during which a lot of players were ill with Delhi belly. In one match, a local batsman, never having seen John Price in action, thought John had a sudden call of nature when he saw him set off in the direction of the sight screen and was taken aback when he smoothly turned round and bounded in towards him. He pulled away convinced that John was intending to run past him to the pavilion – or so folklore has it. I wasn't there you understand.

With two risk-averse captains in Mike Smith and Tom Goddard, the series ended in a turgid draw; this notwithstanding the existence of several exciting batsmen on both sides: Dexter, Barber, Pollock, Bland. They were countered by bores such as Boycott, Barrington, Goddard and Pithey.

Meanwhile, in the Caribbean, the Australians were playing the West Indies for the title 'world champion'. It was an acrimonious series as Richie Benaud, having swapped the ball for the typewriter, had called Griffith a chucker. Bob Simpson and Bill Lawry had a torrid time to begin with, and it was the fourth Test before they asserted themselves with an opening stand of 382. With the rubber decided 2–0 in the home team's favour, the Aussies won the fifth Test. This was Sobers' first series as captain and his batting and bowling form was OK, no more.

Winter passed and as summer arrived in 1965, I looked forward to playing some cricket and watching some first-class cricket. Northern had its own sports ground in Beckenham. No other colleague from Actuarial was interested, but I found someone from the Life Administration Department who was and I went with him in the evening for the pre-season warm up. He looked pretty ancient and I wondered whether he'd be up to it. Looking back, he must have been in his mid-forties. I had no gear, but had bought myself a pair of trainers to wear. I batted first and couldn't lay bat on ball as he was a typical English seamer who first cut the ball this way and then that. I pleaded that I was really a bowler and a number twelve batsman. 'Let us look at your bowling then,' he said. I measured out my run and ambled up and, at the point of delivery, lost control of the ball. I was still trying to spin with the finger which I'd lost in the accident. The surgeon had talked of the phantom finger and I certainly had one for two or three years. So I abandoned pretensions to playing ability. OK ,OK, those that can, do; those that can't write about it.

New Zealand and South Africa were the tourists in 1965 as the MCC tried the innovation of twin tours. I definitely went to Lord's to watch New Zealand, but I cannot honestly say whether my recollections are of matches I actually watched or those I simply saw on television. There was Bert Sutcliffe: neat, busy and orthodox; Sinclair, who seemed to be as short as me and John Edrich scoring a lucky triple century. Of all the Test batsmen I've seen, he'd be the most irritating to bowl to. He regularly played and missed but would obliterate that from his memory and focus on the next delivery.

I particularly wanted to see Fred Trueman and Ted Dexter. Ted had been injured in a car accident so, although I did see him, at Lord's, he was hobbling around the ground on crutches. Ted had tried to get into Parliament as a Tory MP at the general election last October. I assume that the Conservative Central Office did not really rate him. Why else would they ask him to contest a safe Labour seat in Cardiff against James Callaghan? Perhaps they did not want him to give up playing cricket. Ted incidentally is a rare creature: he went to Cambridge but did not get a degree. The finals clashed with the University golf tournament and he preferred a golfing blue to a degree. In 1971, Majid Khan had to choose between playing for Pakistan against England and sitting his finals at Cambridge. He chose the latter.

Fred Trueman I saw once. He still had a beautiful action but none of the aggression I had heard so much about. Much more vivid is the memory of the South Africans. I had my first sighting of Graeme Pollock, nearly as sublime as Gower, but more consistent. On a seamer's pitch at Nottingham and against Tom Cartwright, he had a partnership of 139 with Peter Van der Merwe of which he scored 126. It seems not just incredible but also non-credible. Jim Parks scored 91 to rescue England and was run out by Colin Bland, the ball thrown with an archer's precision, between the running legs of Parks.

In the winter I happened to watch a Spurs football match one Sunday afternoon. I think they were playing Leicester City. I'm not sure why I was watching but I'm glad that I did. Jimmy Greaves scored a sublime goal, snaking past three or four defenders after receiving the ball in his half. I was hooked. As he played for Tottenham, I became a Spurs fan.

A lowlight of that period was the world heavyweight title rematch between Cassius Clay and Sonny Liston. It was one of the first boxing title fights to be televised live. We woke up at 4am to watch it live on poor quality black and white television. We had just about got the reception stabilised when the referee, Joe Walcott stopped the fight. No one, not us nor the commentator knew what was going on.

Muhammad Ali is now an icon and a legend and I now share the same affliction. But in those days I had no time for Cassius Clay whom I considered a loud mouth. I didn't mind him beating my childhood hero Floyd Paterson but I did not like him verbally humiliating a beaten opponent.

3. 1966

I turned twenty-one in February. Life was good, having settled down well in London with a good mixture of Pakistani and English friends. The Northern was a good company to work for and I had a lovely bunch of colleagues to work with. I had a setback in my summer actuarial exams. I entered for three subjects and passed one. But I was not despondent for too long. There was good cricket to watch. Garry Sobers' West Indians were in town. I looked forward to seeing Sobers, Kanhai and Hall in particular.

I watched the Saturday of the MCC *v.* West Indies game. It was a mild day in May and there was a good crowd. Butcher got a century but Sobers, whom I most wanted to see, came in late in the day. During the tea interval, whilst queuing up, someone was listening to the FA Cup Final's commentary on a transistor. Sheffield Wednesday got one and then another and Everton went two-nil down. I thought no more about soccer until I read in the following day's *Times* that Everton won 3–2.

West Indies thrashed England in the First Test, Sobers and Hunte scoring centuries and Lance Gibbs picking up heaps of wickets. Colin Milburn in his first Test got close to a century in the second innings. The selectors rang some changes for the next Test. Captain Mike Smith was sacked and replaced by Colin Cowdrey. Graveney was recalled after a three-year gap, D'Oliviera was given his debut and Boycott and Barry Knight were included in place of Eric Russell and David Allen.

This Lord's Test was the only one I have watched from start to finish. For its ebb and flow it was one of the greatest matches I have seen. I took Thursday, Friday, Monday and Tuesday as holiday. Sunday was a rest day. There was tremendous interest in the game, West Indies had become enormously popular after their exploits under Worrell. I was at the ground at 8.30 for an 11 o'clock start. Or, more accurately, I approached the turnstiles at 8.30. I was staggered at the length of the queue. As I went to find its end, so as to join it, I had to go round three corners and almost reach the turnstiles from the other end. By the time I got in, the West Indians had finished practising at the Nursery End. I saw Sobers, a veritable Adonis, tall, lithe with a gait all his own. I also remember seeing Hall, Kanhai and Rual Branker. Tom Graveney, so often criticised, as Gower would be a decade and a half later, for not showing commitment, belied his reputation, He was practising more assiduously than Boycott. Only half a day's play was possible due to rain. Carew didn't last long and Hunte followed soon after. Kanhai had a frenetic innings of 25. Butcher and Nurse got a decent stand and when rain came again Nurse and Sobers were at the crease. Ken Higgs took three wickets. During stoppages, it was possible to walk right round the ground. I went into the Lord's Museum and saw the stuffed sparrow which had died thirty years previously when its flight path collided with that of a fast delivery bowled by Jehangir Khan, Majid's father. I also went into the bookshop. I'd done the rounds the previous year but how can one tire of history?

The following day I set off early hoping for better weather and again reached the ground at 8.30. The queue was as long as on the first day and at nearly half past ten, as I got to within a few yards of the turnstile, I went to get my wallet from my jacket pocket – yes it was jackets and trousers for watching cricket. To my consternation, I had left my wallet at home. I felt my trouser pocket and found that my total accessible wealth was ten shillings. The ticket for the day's play was six shillings so I'd have four shillings for grub and any purchases such as the Programme and scorecard. It wasn't just that, I hated not having money on me in case something unexpected happened. I was on the point of abandoning the queue to go back home when my alter ego said, 'Don't be silly, don't miss the cricket.' I had occasionally fasted during the month of Ramzan so the solution was simple. I'd skip food and drink.

So that was that, I paid and entered the ground and found myself a suitable seat. Shortly afterwards a Sri Lankan came and sat next to me. I think his name was Pereira although that's a bit like saying I know an Irishman called Murphy. He was as garrulous as I was reticent. We got talking as the game progressed with West Indies resuming their innings. He took out an enormous flask and poured himself coffee.

'Would you like some?' he asked me.

'No, I'm alright,' I replied.

We watched cricket for a while before he got talking again. 'What do you do?' he asked.

'I'm a student.'

'What are you studying?'

'I'm studying to be an actuary.'

'What is that?'

Explaining what they do is a perennial problem for actuaries. So I said, 'Well you know what accountancy is?'

'Of course I do.'

'Well the accountant and the actuary both work in the field of finance but we do different things. Accountants record what happened in the past, how much money you've made in the last year, how much you've spent and what the current position is.'

'I know that, but what do you do?'

'We look to the future. We predict what you'd make in the future, how much you'd spend and what is likely to be left.'

'I see, I can use you.'

'Well, I used the word "you" in the general sense. We normally work for insurance companies and pension funds and it is corporate wealth that we make predictions on.'

'So you're not really like an accountant.'

'Not at all. Accountants are always right and we are nearly always wrong.'

'So you're not as good as them?'

'No, they deal in facts so the scope for error is small. if the figures are checked. When you make predictions, there are so many variables that, it would be sheer fluke if you got all of them right.' We were rabbiting on because of an interruption in play owing to rain.

'You haven't drunk all morning. Here have a cup.'

This time I accepted. He must do this regularly as he had a spare cup.

'You didn't tell me what you do? Are you a student too?' It was a silly question as he looked twice my age.

'Good lord, no, my student days are over. I'm a doctor.'

'It takes five years doesn't it? Ours is about that long too.'

'Yes, we learn 10,000 new words.'

'All tongue twisters.'

He told me that he went to Colombo's top school. I've forgotten the name he gave me, but it must be the one that, three decades later, Jayawardene and Sangakarra went to.

I tried to concentrate on the cricket but he continued to talk. Although a Sri Lankan, he seemed to be similar to a typical Indian or Pakistani, a natural show-off in front of strangers. He talked of having two houses in Sri Lanka (one in Colombo and one in Kandy) and two in London. In an effort to shut him up, I said I'd lived in ten houses, neglecting to mention that they were all rented. Then there was his tea plantation and an uncle who was a minister.

As the lunch interval approached, he opened his canvas bag (rucksacks were unknown then) and took out of it a mountain of sandwiches. Again he offered me some and again I declined. Again he insisted and again I gave in. I then explained that I'd left my wallet at home.

'That won't happen to me,' he said. 'My wife always says, "Don't forget your wallet" when I'm about to leave.'

'I must remember to get married,' I said.

She always packs a week's worth of lunch whenever I go to a cricket match.'

They were all meat sandwiches bathed in black pepper and really hot. I never saw him again after that day, not during that match nor at any time in the future.

West Indies were all out for 269 and Boycott and Milburn went out to open for England. I wanted to see Wes Hall open the bowling for West Indies but no, it was Sobers himself who did that. And what a lyrical experience that was. Off an angular run, he glided in a rhythmical approach, like a well-greased locomotive that was travelling at the speed that optimises the output to input ratio. It must be difficult for any batsman who faces Sobers for the first time. His run-up gives no advance warning of the speed at which the ball is propelled in your direction. And what a contrast Wes Hall provided from the other end! He bounded in off a very long run-up, the earth trembling beneath his feet, his shirt, unbuttoned to his navel, billowing in the breeze, sweat on his jet black chest glistening in the sun and providing a stark contrast to his white shirt and teeth, a golden crucifix beating against his chest, rebounding and beating again, his eyes fixed at the point where he wants the ball to land, but so eager that the eye-stalks seemed ready to pop out, in the way Louis Armstrong's always did. The sheer physical energy was intimidating and that's before the fast thunderbolts were unleashed. Milburn went cheaply. That brought in Graveney who was in commanding form. It was fascinating to watch two contrasts. The first was Hall's unbridled and intimidating energy being repelled with unhurried elegance; the second was the differences in the batting styles of Graveney and Boycott, the artist versus the artisan. Graveney's game was on a different plane and it made you wonder why his career had been so intermittent. Anyway, these two had a long stand. Graveney, who took a painful blow on the thumb, was unlucky to fall for 96. Early on Saturday morning, Sobers again opened the bowling and completely hoodwinked Barrington with a wicked delivery that swung in and then moved away after landing. D'Oliviera, playing his first Test innings, looked comfortable and played some pleasing strokes before disaster struck. Parks drove Hall straight back and the ball crashed into the stumps dislodging the bails. D'Oliviera was well out of his crease. He thought that was that, his innings was over. It was not, of course, and Hall had the presence of mind to uproot a stump. Jim Parks made 91 and England had a lead of 86.

One of the joys of this Test match was the enthusiasm of London's Caribbean community who came to support West Indies. Boisterous but humorous and sporting, they made cricket watching doubly enjoyable. As I recall it, everyone was wearing jacket and tie. There was one character who was flying the Barbadian flag. When, on the final morning, West Indies were losing a flurry of wickets he put on a glum face and lowered the flag to half mast. When they were 95 for 5, effectively 9 for 5 because they'd conceded a lead of 86 in the first innings, he lowered the flag completely and, on another pole raised the Union Jack. In that crisis position, David Holford came in to join his cousin, Sobers. There was no mid-pitch conversation between the two, no attempt by Garry to shield Holford from the attack. Cowdrey kept trying to give Sobers singles to attack Holford, and Sobers kept taking them. There were no further successes before lunch. After lunch Sobers accelerated and got to his century. He was followed by Holford. 269 runs they had put together. By then our Caribbean friend had raised the Barbadian flag and lowered the Union Jack.

When Sobers reached his century a couple of supporters dashed on to the field and one of them lifted him with a bear hug from behind. Later they did the same to Holford. When Sobers declared, England had a mini-collapse before Graveney, who'd been held back because of his thumb injury, joined Milburn. He held one end up while Milburn bludgeoned his way to a century. When he got there, three or four English supporters rushed on to the field and attempted to lift him from behind. Such was his weight and girth that they could not do so.

Sobers was in magnificent form that summer. Statistically it was his best series ever: over 700 runs at an average of over 100, twenty-one wickets and umpteen catches, not to mention winning all five tosses. I doubt if there has ever been a better, all-round performance, even Noble in 1903/4, Armstrong in 1920/1, Miller in 1950/1, Sobers in 1963 or 1964/5, Botham in 1978 or 1979 or 1979/80 or 1981, Imran in 1982, 1982/3 or 1987.

I watched Sobers a lot that summer, either at the ground or on television. For an attacking batsman he had an impregnable defence. He gave the impression, as no other batsman I've seen did, that he would never get out other than, to borrow an insurance jargon, through an Act of God. Only divine intervention could disturb the progress of this genius.

At the Oval, such intervention did happen, God using Brian Close, his fearless agent on earth. The selectors had axed Colin Cowdrey and in his place made Brian captain. It was his first Test for a while. At first it was normal service. West Indies lost four wickets cheaply before Kanhai and Sobers had one of their curiously few century stands together. Kanhai got a century but Sobers this time made only 81 and the team's total was 268. That seemed sufficient when England teetered at 166 for seven. At that point John Murray, who'd come in, in place of Jim Parks, joined Graveney and the two put on over 200 before Murray was out for 121. Graveney went on to get 165. But that was not the end of it, Snow and Higgs put on 128 for the last wicket. Trailing by over 250 runs West Indies lost wickets steadily. Sobers was out first ball caught by Close at silly, no, stupid short leg. Close unflinchingly kept his eyes on the ball when Sobers swung at a short pitched delivery. England won by an innings. Sobers' graciousness in defeat, which we thought nothing of at the time, today contrasts with the surliness of Illingworth, who was playing in this match, when he was the losing captain seven years later.

I took part in an inter-departmental cricket match. Actuarial, being a small department were short of players. An unassuming clerk, a ginger haired Yorkshireman called Pete McRobert, said, 'I'll play, if you're short of players.' Beggars can't be choosers, so he was drafted in.

Our opponents got around 120 and we won by five wickets. Pete went in at number five and scored an unbeaten seventy-nine.

'I didn't know you could bat?' I said to him.

'I told you I was a batsman not a bowler.'

'I know you did, but you didn't say you could bat. I say I'm a bowler but I can't bowl.'

'I played for All England Schools against Public Schools at Lords; had trials for Yorkshire. I would have got a contract after a year in the 2nd XI but my family couldn't afford to support me.'

He didn't stay long with us and went into Civil Service.

It wasn't all cricket of course. This was the year we won the soccer world cup. I watched on television with all the passion of a new convert. I had no idea of the nuances of the game or of the relative strengths of the teams but lapped up the opinions of the *Times* correspondents. I adored Jimmy Greaves, Bobby Charlton, Bobby Moore, Martin Peters and Alan Ball. Our football in the early stages was utilitarian rather than exciting. Not many believed Alf Ramsey when he said England would win the cup. Brazil did not fire, Pele being hacked out of the game, North Korea was the surprise package but the team that really caught the eye was Portugal. Their Eusebio was the star of the tournament, but they lost to England in the semi.

When England got to the final, played on 29th June, the day before the Third Test started, Alf Ramsey preferred Roger Hunt to Jimmy Greaves. As a victory for mechanical efficiency over genius, it was on the same scale as Gooch dropping Gower a quarter of a century later. Incensed, I nearly withdrew my support.

It was a thrilling match, set up by an early goal conceded by Ray Wilson. If watching Test cricket is a cerebral experience then watching football is an emotional one.

For the next ten years I followed Tottenham, often going to matches with my mate Allen Kelly, a Chelsea season-ticket holder. Spurs had quite a side: Alan Gilzean, so big and yet so dainty; Cliff Jones with winged heels; the industrious Terry Venables; Dave Mackay, the skipper; the wonderful Pat Jennings with a deep deep voice and enormous hands and later Martin Chivers.

In the winter I joined evening classes to play squash. The coach was a cockney with an Australian wife. In practice there was no coaching but we just played. It was there that Naseem met Jill and it wasn't long before they were courting.

It wasn't all pleasure; there was work and studies; or perhaps there wasn't. I took three subjects in the summer exams and passed just one. At work I had been transferred from Quotations, where some contact was maintained with the branches and brokers to the Surrender Values section, where we spent all our time calculating surrender values on policies assigned to banks. It was crying out for computerisation. We had an A5-sized card for each policy. Included in the Northern group of companies were London and Scottish (one company) and Scottish Metropolitan, both taken over by the Northern some 30–40 years previously and closed to new business. Some of their policyholders were born as long ago as 1870 and had not paid a premium for decades. Most probably they were dead but 'Ours is not to reason why', if the Bank wants an up-to-date surrender value, we must give it to them.

To make the work interesting we set ourselves production targets. Also, we used to get our manual or semi-automatic calculation machines to beat out rhythms which it would do if it had a recurrent pattern in the answer. For example

$1/6^{th}$ i.e. 0.166666666… has one sort of rhythm, a boring one;

$1/7^{th}$ i.e. 0.142857142857142857.. has a more complex one

$1/11^{th}$ i.e. .09090909.. had an interesting staccato rhythm

Who was it that said the devil finds work for idle minds?

When I was in Quotations, the occasional juicy bit of gossip came our way when a celebrity proposed for insurance. There was a pop singer whose manager had taken out a large life assurance policy on his life and it came to us to set a price for the risk. He had gone for a detailed medical which we scanned for juice. It turned out that he contracted VD every time he did a season in Blackpool. I told Colin about it and, as a man who'd seen it all, he said that wasn't unusual.

We also saw some estate planning, estate duty being a bigger menace than its successor, inheritance tax, is today. One of these was for Ted Dexter's father. One of my colleagues, Alan Platten, became quite adept at it and it wasn't long before he became the director of a broker who specialised in it. Another colleague, Joe Soap, tried to do the same. He spoke engagingly on the phone and was extremely persuasive. Brian Dawson, our overall boss, happened to hear one such conversation and was extremely alarmed because the advice was completely wrong. He called the errant clerk into his cubicle gave him a dressing down and said that the next time the client phoned he wanted to speak to him. Well, the client did phone and the call was transferred to Brian. But she wouldn't speak to him.

'I want to speak to Joe Soap.'

'I'm Brian Dawson, I'm Joe's Manager.'

'I want to speak to Joe.'

'I appreciate that but I wanted to explain that some of the things he told you were, well, wrong.'

'Mr Soap understands what I want. I'll only speak to him.'

'But I must correct wrong advice he has given you.'

'If I can't speak to Mr Soap I'll take my business elsewhere.'

'That's your choice.'

Indeed it was and that is what she did.

One of the unusual policies that we used to issue was called Issue Risk policy. If a man places his estate in trust for the benefit of, say, his widow and his children, and children's children, then a bar to dividing up the estate is the possibility that there may be children unknown or children born in the future. As to the former, the executors would issue notices asking any bastards to come forward but the latter remained a problem. So they could take out an insurance policy which would pay out if a child were to be born in the future. To prevent this being money for old rope (for the insured) we used to make sure that (a) the couple were happily married and (b) that the wife was past child-bearing age.

Looking back, I led a schizophrenic existence. There were two of me: one who was training to be an actuary, worked at the Northern with a great circle of friends, mostly English; the other lived in Cricklewood with a Pakistani family and a mostly Pakistani circle of friends with a few Indian ones as well. Coursing through my veins was a love for music and cricket. None of my Pakistani friends cared much for cricket. What we had in common was a love for music and films and food, although eating out was a rarity. Naseem's mother was a great cook. Pakistani students in England in those days spent all their time discussing Pakistani politics, although my closest friends Naseem and Ali Jafari were apolitical.

4. 1967

Spurs got to the cup final where they were due to meet Chelsea. I was desperately keen to go, but figured that the local Derby would be a sell-out and I didn't want to pay black market rates; not as a matter of principle but on cost grounds. As it turned out, most people thought the same and the touts had a bad day. I watched the match on television and it never came to life.

During the summer of 1967's actuarial examination, I sat for three papers and passed all of them. Suddenly, at the age of twenty-two, I was an Associate of the Institute of Actuaries. Two more subjects and I'd be a Fellow. But I was evolving as a person and my priorities were changing. It would be another four years before I became an actuary. I had a circle of friends from work: Kevin Phillips, Colin Coles and his girlfriend Sandy Girling, Allen Kelly, Eric McGill and Mashuque Rehman. Mashuque was from what was then East Pakistan, now Bangladesh. He was in his late twenties and although part of our circle, a tad more mature than us. He liked his drink and when drunk, would be very verbally aggressive towards me. The sight of me sober offended him.

Another good friend from work was Peter Wilson, who looked like David McCallum, the actor who played Ilya Kuriyakin in *The Man from U.N.C.L.E.* He was a lovely man, slightly snobbish, wearing thirty-five guinea suits. He was my friend but he wasn't everyone's favourite. He was married and our contact was usually at work although we did meet some weekends. He introduced me to opera and to Spanish guitar music, particularly Rodrigo's Guitar Concerto. I was so captivated by the concerto that I resolved to learn to play Spanish guitar. I enrolled in an evening class and bought myself a guitar, for the princely sum of £30 which doesn't seem a lot but was three weeks take-home pay. Every week I went on the No 16 bus to attend evening classes held in a school near Edgware Road Station, to be taught by a Mr Mitchell. Being left-handed I wanted the string order to be reversed. Mr Mitchell said that as both hands are used it should not matter. But try as I would, I couldn't strum with my right hand, so eventually he allowed me to swap the strings round. The next problem was tuning. I couldn't do it. I don't think I'm tone deaf. If someone plays or sings the wrong note I can tell. But tuning the strings, well, I couldn't do it. It was OK in the class as the teacher would do it for me. The problem was practising at home. After forty-five minutes of trying to tune the first string to E, you get more and more confused. (It's a bit like having your eyes tested. 'Is this lens better than the previous one?') My resolve was broken and I gave up. When a couple of young men found out that I was travelling every Thursday with a guitar in hand (don't ask me how they happened to be on the same bus every week) they started mocking me, calling me John Lennon and singing, 'He's got a ticket to ride'. I quietly abandoned any aspirations to be a guitarist.

Peter died in the mid-seventies from a brain tumour.

Mike Woodburn was another good friend, but we did not often socialise as he had a steady supply of girlfriends. Timekeeping was a problem for him so he evolved his own system. He lived in Putney and used to shave at night and lay out his work wear on a chair. He slept in the altogether, got up at 8.15, didn't bother with the bathroom but put on his work wear and managed to be at the tube station by 8.20 – or so he said. Colin and Sandy apart, the rest of us were single and, Mike apart, if we were looking for female company at all we weren't letting on. Colin moved to Friends Provident late in 1966 so I didn't see him on a daily basis. The rest of us spent a lot of time during the week in each other's company, and leisure activities, cricket, music, etc. took precedence over studies. Kevin had already packed it in. I also gradually became left wing in my politics and came to believe that the City did nothing useful. Weekends were usually spent in the company of Naseem and other Pakistani friends.

I mention all this to explain why in 1968 and 1969 I did not pass any subject in the actuarial exams. But because I had already passed eight out of the ten subjects, I knew that it was a lack of application rather than a lack of ability that held me back. Not so for Allen Kelly (two years older than me) and Eric McGill (eight days younger than me). Both had been to university so, when we got together, they were just starting out while I had several exams under my belt. When, like me they started failing, they did not have the same emotional reassurance of having passed some. Both abandoned actuarial careers when both were bright enough to be actuaries.

But I'm getting ahead of myself. What was I talking about? Ah yes leisure. The Northern organised a fifty-mile London (Westminster Bridge) to Brighton walk and some 170 took part including Kevin, Colin, Eric, Allen and me. We never seriously expected to finish the journey so we didn't pace ourselves or conserve our energy. (I recall simulating Wesley Hall's bowling action on the South Circular). When we got to Coulsdon, the first checkpoint, the proper walkers merely consumed and expelled fluids and set off again without tarrying. Kevin and I on the other hand gorged ourselves on sandwiches and drinks and set off half an hour later, but I could hardly move. Muscle and bone in my legs seemed to have turned to stone. I could barely put one leg in front of the other. Eventually I gave up at either Reigate or Redhill, I can't remember which. It took me fifteen minutes to go up the stairs at the railway station. By then the fast walkers had already completed the course and were fêted by the Chief Executive, to use modern jargon, I think he was called the General Manager. In all, eleven completed the course, out of 170 starters. One of them was a ruddy faced and busty lass, the kind referred to as earthy or rustic or a country girl. She was the only girl to complete it and was singled out for lavish praise. It turned out later that she got a lift from a lorry driver for practically half the journey.

In 1967 India and Pakistan were touring England, India first. Incidentally, Kevin was the only friend who regularly watched cricket with me. None of my Pakistani friends had more than a passing interest in it.

The weather was dreadful when Kevin and I saw India play Middlesex. My only recollection is of Farook Engineer opening the batting after tea. He had recently scored 94 before lunch on the opening day of a Test against West Indies so I was expecting style and flair. I was seated in line with the square leg umpire and remember thinking how ugly his stance was. He had his legs wide apart and he stooped so much that his bottom stuck out in a most unbecoming way. Thank God it was 94 and not a century before lunch. He was not fit to join the august company of Trumper, Macartney and Bradman (and, in 1976, Majid Khan).

In the first Test Boycott scored a double century but was dropped for batting too slowly. Over the forty-odd years that I've been watching the game there are only a handful of cricketers that I have detested and Boycott was one of them; Hanif another. I hate selfishness in a team game. Boycott had run out at key moments both Dexter (against South Africa in 1964/5) and Barber (against Australia in 1966/7). Brian Lara and Kevin Pietersen are two modern batsmen I dislike. All successful people are selfish, it is a question of degree.

In a wet summer, India suffered from not having fast bowlers (the reserve wicket-keeper opened the bowling once). They had a quartet of high-class spinners, but they were handicapped by a wet ball, poor fielding and having too few runs to play with. Chandu Borde their star batsman, having recently scored two centuries against the mighty West Indies, hardly got a run whilst Dilip Sardesai, the most promising of the younger batsman, seldom played. In the first Test, faced with a huge first-innings deficit, Pataudi decided to lead by example and scored a magnificent 148. It avoided an innings defeat but not defeat. Brian Close was the captain; Ray Illingworth was preferred to Fred Titmus and David Allen. With twenty wickets in three Tests, he had his best series.

Still, if the Indians were a pushover, would the Pakistanis provide sterner competition? They had in Majid Jehangir (later Majid Khan) and Asif Iqbal, two players who'd excelled the previous winter against the MCC Under 25s captained by Mike Brearley. Alas, as they went round the counties, their bowling kept getting hammered. Middlesex toyed with them.

I saw the first day of the match against Surrey. After the early loss of a wicket, Majid batted with great panache to score 60. The left-handed Ghulam Abbas, a cousin of Zaheer Abbas, played one cracking off-drive before getting out. After that we had the interminable monotony of Hanif Mohammed. At the end of the day I hung around the pavilion and saw Majid in cheerful form, Saeed Ahmed busy with his wife and not really part of the team.

My concentration was broken by the sound of a booming and familiar voice. I turned round to find a tall man in a beige summer suit, a prominent nose, eyebrows that needed cutting and, underneath them, eyes that were darting from one corner to another. It was Brian Johnston, checking to see how many of the crowd present had noticed him. He provided a striking contrast to Qamaruddin Butt, the prolific author of several books on Pakistan cricket, none of which were proof-read, who stood silent and unnoticed, a portable typewriter and a sheaf of paper in hand.

Hanif, the captain, was so worried about his bowling resources for the first Test that he called upon four bowlers not in the squad. On the stroke of lunch, Intikhab Alam bowled Eric Russell with a googly the batsman offered no shot to. The rest of the day saw solid professional English batting against mediocre bowling. There was a lot of rain about to interrupt play. On the second day, when Pakistan batted, wickets fell steadily; Majid was caught and bowled by Robin Hobbs. At least this was better than 1962, we were being clinically taken apart rather than being pulverised.

I had persuaded many of my work colleagues to come and watch 'the highly talented cricketers from Pakistan who will teach the English how to play the game they'd invented'. They came on Saturday. My boss Dave Reynolds, a lovely man, came, as did Colin and Sandy, Kevin, Allen and Eric. It was a bleak day, the sun hiding behind the clouds and it was always threatening to rain. Pakistan lost two wickets within the first ten minutes and Asif Iqbal, considered to be a bowler who could bat, came into join Hanif. He immediately hit a four and Hanif came down the pitch and spoke to him, no doubt to say, 'We'll get them in dot balls'. Thereafter they had a soporific stand. Eric, who arrived fifteen minutes late complained, 'What a dull day? No fours, no wickets.' At one stage Illingworth lost hold of the slippery ball and it dropped at rank long-hop length and trickled a few feet before coming to rest. As it was a legal delivery Asif walked up to and, it in much the same way a golfer would address a tee shot, hit it to long on. The ball sped away to the boundary. Again, Hanif ambled down the pitch to admonish Asif. I was reminded of Sir Toby Belch saying to Malvolio in *Twelfth Night*, 'Do you think because you are virtuous there shall be no more cakes and ale?'

Colin and Sandy, love birds, did not join us for lunch as they'd brought their own food. The rest of us, for some reason, went outside in search of a restaurant rather than stick with what was available at the ground. We walked back in the direction of the tube station and found an Indian restaurant on Acacia Road. For want of anything better we went in. Neither Dave nor Allen would touch curry and stuck to omelettes. They complained that the omelettes were hot. Perhaps the cook used the same frying pan. We returned late from lunch to be greeted by 'You haven't missed anything, no fours, no wickets.' I think play stopped around tea-time and that was it.

On Monday, when running out of partners, Hanif at last attacked. I'm told it was splendid stuff although I wasn't there to see it. He ended with an unbeaten 187, his first Test century in England. He played four more innings in this series and managed only another 41 runs in total.

In the second Test Pakistan got thrashed. Surprisingly, Saeed Ahmed top scored in both innings on a seaming wicket. Majid failed again. During the sixties, fans had low expectations of the Pakistan cricket team so this did not surprise me and I was prepared for the worst at the Oval in the third and final Test. In the event, my eldest sister was getting married, in August in Somalia, where my father was on a three-year UN assignment. I tried hard to have it postponed but to no avail. In the end, as the elder brother, I had to go. At least I did something useful when I was there. As the proud owner of a Yashika SLR camera, I kept clicking to take wedding photographs. My sister was grateful for these as none of those taken by the official photographer came out. He had failed to take his lens cap off. However, I missed the two highlights of the Pakistan tour: Majid Khan's 147 in 61 minutes against Glamorgan and the 190 run stand in the Oval Test between Asif Iqbal and Intikhab Alam.

Those weren't the only sensations I missed. Brian Close, who'd led England with aggression and cunning (his own aggression and Illingworth's cunning, if the latter is to be believed) was sacked because of some alleged time-wasting in a county match against Warwickshire. So the captaincy for the winter tour to the Caribbean went to Cowdrey, yes, to the man who'd said 'Maybe' when someone asked if he was indecisive.

It had been known for some time that the Northern would shift its Head Office to East Croydon and that day arrived late in 1967. I've never understood why Croydon, which is practically outer London. Why not go much further out? Anyway it presented me with a problem. I lived in Cricklewood in north-west London with a wonderful family and I didn't want to move. I had some great colleagues at the Northern and I didn't want to lose them either.

The early omens weren't good. I was told that I had to go to London Bridge to get to East Croydon. When I got to London Bridge, I was told that I should go to Platform 5, so I did. A train was about to leave so I caught it. Half an hour later with no sight of East Croydon, I asked a passenger and was told that I was on the wrong train. I got off at Beckenham, deep in Kent. I checked how best to get to East Croydon and took a bus. I was 90 minutes late.

Luckily, I found that I could go to East Croydon from Victoria. If I caught the No. 16 bus from Cricklewood at 8am, I would reach Victoria Station by 8.25, enabling me to catch the 8.33 to East Croydon from there and make the office by 9.00, just. So I stayed. As it was impractical to go to the Institute of Actuaries during the three study half-days every week, the Northern arranged a spare room, the 'study room' for use by us students. It was right next to the Valuation Department. Whereas in the Institute library silence was mandatory so you had to study, in the office study room, it was difficult not to talk.

There was a local landlord who owned a number of condemned houses near the railway station which he would let to students and foreigners, i.e. people without clout. How he managed to stay on the right side of the law no one knows. Mashuque rented a room in one such house. The place was disgusting. One could put up with the bare wires or even with faulty wiring, the earth being live and the neutral earth, but a lack of basic hygiene was unacceptable. I remember once using the toilet he shared with other tenants. I flushed only to find the water level rising in the wash basin, yes wash basin, and almost overflowing with the stuff I was trying to flush.

During the winter months, every Friday evening we had a concert in Mashuque's room. A colleague, Geoff Jackson, had a vast collection of pop singles and classical LPs. He provided the programme and the music. He would start with an overture, followed by a concerto and end with a symphony. Mashuque offered tea and biscuits. Biscuits we didn't mind but we were too scared to drink the tea, fearing that the water might have been passed by us.

One day after work Allen asked me if I was interested in coming to a talk. I was game and he explained on the way that there was an American off-shoot of Christianity called Scientology and one of their people was giving a talk on it. Allen said he wouldn't give his views on them and said we should listen to the talk without pre-conceptions. There were a fair number of people in the room, enough to merit the 'House Full' tag that they'd placed on the door. I can't remember whether we were vetted before entry, but you certainly had to say who you were if you had a question. Allan was the third or fourth person to ask a question. The question was an inquisitive one, seeking to better understand their beliefs and objectives, whereas some of the earlier questions were sycophantic and quite possibly planted. The speaker said, 'You're obviously here to make trouble not to learn. Please leave the room.' Allen pleaded that he'd come to learn but the speaker would have none of it. Allen had to go when a couple of heavies walked menacingly in his direction. So we left convinced that it was a 'brainwashing set up'.

By now I'd become a regular pub-goer as it was a common meeting place for the gang. The Railway Tavern just outside East Croydon station was our most frequent haunt. My tipple was cider. One day we were joined by a colleague, three or four years older than me of slightly below average height with a large forehead made even larger by two deep frontal recesses in his hair. Upwardly mobile, he normally had a stockbroker accent but, if you heard him talking on the phone to his wife you would hear him lapsing into his native Irish lilt. He would never shirk a challenge. We got talking about pubs losing beer mugs and wondered why people would steal them and then how. He said, 'Easy, you put it in your coat pocket and sneak out.'

'A pint mug is too big for a coat pocket.'

'No, it isn't.'

'OK, you show us how.'

He quickly finished his pint and then spent the best part of twenty minutes trying to force the mug into the pocket of his large blue coat. Some of us acted as scouts in case a barmaid came. He had great difficulty (it was a bit like labour in reverse) but, to the sound of ripping material, he managed to force it in. That wasn't the end of it. To complete the dare he had to leave the pub. He did it, concealing the pocket with his briefcase. When he was five yards out of the pub, with a triumphant look on his face he pulled the mug out but had to apply such force that when the mug broke free from the pocket it flew out of his hand and crashed on the pavement. All pretty juvenile stuff, from someone pushing thirty.

On Saturdays we often went to Piccadilly Circus to loiter and to play the fruit machines eventually ending up in some bar. I was teetotal – well, cider didn't count – but the company was good. We used to play a game called matchsticks. Each of us was given three matchsticks. Each player had to hide in a clenched fist 0, 1, 2 or 3 matchsticks. Each of us then had to guess the total number of matchsticks held clenched. If four of us were playing the total could be any whole number from 0 to 12. Whoever guessed correctly dropped out and the survivors played another round. So it went on until only one was left. He'd be the loser and typically paid for everyone's meal. Eric reckoned that he had cracked the game and challenged us to a game, the prize being steaks for all at the Aberdeen Angus. Alas he lost. I felt a tug on my shirt and saw him looking at me and saying, 'Can I see you in the toilet?'

I wondered what he was playing at. The fact was that he was so confident of winning that he had not brought sufficient funds with him. He wanted a loan.

Ever since he saw *Women in Love,* Kevin had a crush on Glenda Jackson. One weekend when we were in town he wanted to see the latest film, a biography of Tchaikovsky with Richard Chamberlain in the lead role and Glenda as his nymphomaniac wife. We tried to get tickets but the eight o'clock show was booked up. He persuaded me to go for the eleven pm showing and we booked tickets. That left four hours to kill so we saw another film, *Lion In Winter.* It must have been around half past one when the second film ended. I can't recall how we went home.

One evening the four of us, Kevin, Allen, Eric and I were in Leicester Square, probably seeing a film and then we looked for a restaurant to have a meal. We saw the *Guinea and the Piggee*, where for a guinea you could make a pig of yourself. We went in only to be thrown out with an 'I'm sorry we're fully booked,' excuse. We looked through the window and concluded that if they're fully booked, most of the customers were invisible. Allen thought it was racial discrimination as Kevin and I were Asians. Anyway, after some haggling we gave up and went to another restaurant. We took our time over the meal. Suddenly Kevin realised that it was 12.15. He quickly caught a cab to Victoria and all of us (except Eric who'd already gone home).piled into the cab. Once it got to Victoria, Kevin and Allen disappeared. I'd missed the last tube and the last bus, to Cricklewood. Nor could I find a cab willing to take me home. There were plenty of American tourists who were easier to fleece, and who gave tips. So at around one am, I set off on foot with a vague idea of the route. I got to Hyde Park and walked round its perimeter until I reached Marble Arch. From there it was a straight line, the Edgware Road. It was around three am before I got home. I was lucky that the front door wasn't bolted from the inside. Today it is unthinkable that anyone would sleep without bolting the front door from the inside but those were innocent and tranquil days. I genuinely believed that white men didn't burgle. Naseem's mother would often leave the front door key under the doormat.

I can't believe that I've got this far without mentioning tennis. I used to follow it as a kid. Ken Rosewall was my favourite and after him Neil Fraser and Rod Laver, both left-handers like me. When I came to England the quality of tennis at Wimbledon was low as anyone who was any good had turned professional. Every year Roy Emerson beat Fred Stolle in the final. Strange to hear that they shared rooms on the circuit. Fred must have been sick of the sight of Roy. This year we had the languid Spaniard Manuel Santana beat an atypical German, Wilhelm Bangert.

I had an interesting experience at the Annual General Meeting of Northern's Chess Club. After the formal meeting there were sandwiches and sausage rolls and tea and coffee. After that we had a game of lightning chess. I was drawn against the General Manager of the Accident Department, a senior man and a serious chess player. It was called lightning chess as only 10 seconds were allowed per move. A slow thinker like me stood no chance and within five minutes I was a move away from extinction. Then the compère said,

'OK, from now on black is white and white is black.'

You should have seen the expression on my opponent's face. He was on the brink of check-mating me; instead he'd handed it on a plate to me.

Ali Jafari, whom I'd seen only intermittently, as he was doing a post graduate course in Edinburgh, came down to work for Marconi in Chelmsford. We had many common interests such as love of music, poetry and jokes. We spent a lot of time together. I remember going with him to meet a friend of his in Epping who had a vast collection of country and western music.

5. 1968

1968 was an Ashes year. Bill Lawry was bringing an in-transition team. Would we be able to overcome them and regain the Ashes? They seemed particularly weak in bowling, relying exclusively upon Garth Mackenzie. They had a mystery bowler, Gleeson, but we wondered whether that was hype.

Test matches weren't the only cricket I was interested in. For the first time, counties were allowed to register overseas players without residence qualification. A number of overseas stars were snapped up, Garry Sobers by Nottinghamshire, Rohan Kanhai by Warwickshire, Clive Lloyd and Farook Engineer by Lancashire, Majid Khan by Glamorgan, Asif Iqbal by Kent. Later Surrey signed Intikhab Alam. Although I lived in Middlesex and had seen the odd county match, the Middlesex team, boasting several Test players, Fred Titmus, Peter Parfitt, Eric Russell, John Murray as well as future Test players, Mike Brearley and Clive Radley, never interested me. Brearley in his autobiography (*The Art of Captaincy*) talked of cliques within the team. I tended to go to the Oval instead.

Majid took some time to get going. A succession of single figure scores were disappointing. Still he played several important knocks in Glamorgan's valiant but ultimately unavailing title chase. Sobers made an immediate impact on the fortunes of Nottinghamshire. His personal performance was less sensational than he achieved five years earlier for South Australia. Instead he transformed the attitude of the players. A gambler by instinct, he had the previous winter lost a Test match by setting England an over generous target. In the county championship he made some bold declarations. Mind you his interest in gambling wasn't confined to the cricket field. He was an avid student of horse racing. One of the key tasks of the Notts' twelfth man was to run to the bookies and place the skipper's bet. One day the accumulator bet that Sobers had selected came off and Sobers waited in the evening for the twelfth man to return with the winnings, a bumper amount. There was only one snag. The twelfth man had forgotten to place the bet. The dressing room braced itself for a blast from the skipper. Sobers' face registered disappointment and misery but not for long. Soon he burst into a smile, 'What the heck, its only money,' he said.

Unusually, cricket competed for my attention with tennis, at least it did during the Wimbledon fortnight. For the first time it was open to professionals and we had stars from a different brighter galaxy. Some of them were on the wane. I mean, think of Pancho Gonzales, the brightest star of the late forties and the fifties, now aged forty. He didn't get very far in the singles. My boyhood hero Ken Rosewall got further but didn't make it to the final in which two southpaws fought it out. Rod Laver emerged victor and Tony Roche was runner up. Billie-Jean King won the ladies' title.

My attention to sport was distracted by events at work. One morning Eric, who was supposed to be studying in the study-room came running saying, 'Come on, lets all take out with profits life assurance policies.'

'Why?' I asked him.

'Valuation Department have been asked to carry out an urgent valuation of the company. This is summer, not the year end, so they must be valuing the company because somebody's trying to buy it.'

We pondered the significance of the remark. If they closed Northern's with profits business, which was of no interest to the shareholders, then the money set aside for any future calamities would gradually be released as the policies matured, so high bonuses could be expected. One by one, all of us filled out a proposal for the most expensive with profits endowment we could afford. Mine was for a premium of £150 per year, quite a large sum when you bear in mind that my gross salary was around £1,000. The Deputy Actuary of the Northern came to hear of this and called us all in to say that he was not aware that the company was up for sale (which might have been true), so do not take out policies unless you can afford it. One by one we all withdrew our applications. Six months later the Northern did get taken over by Commercial Union and a further six months later the with profits business was closed. A little digging around showed that the Deputy Actuary and a young high flying actuary had taken out with profits policies on the lives of their children.

The takeover was, to use the city jargon, a hostile one. The stuffees' management did not wish to be stuffed by the stuffor. Commercial Union's General Manager, Eric Orbell went on a charm offensive. He went over the heads of Northern's management and talked to us plebs. He lifted his trousers and showed a pair of socks.

'Do you know what these are? I'll tell you, they're socks. Do you know who sold them? I'll tell you it was Marks and Spencer. Have you seen them before? I bet you have, Marks and Spencer are the largest sellers of socks in the UK and this is their highest selling design. Marks and Spencer are so successful because they put the customer first and the shareholder a close second.'

I thought to myself, 'Why does he need us, if he answers his own questions? Rather like a hermaphrodite, he's self sufficient.' I didn't like him, my colleagues didn't like him and our management didn't like him. However, the shareholders did and the takeover went through. Most of the senior management lost their jobs. Our head office in Croydon was going to be closed down and we'd have to move into CU's head office in 66 Cheapside.

We knew that the very special bond between us was going to be broken. It seemed inevitable that some of would move on and form new friendships. I knew this only too well. Every time Dad's job changed we had to move and friendships that I thought would last for ever, had to be compromised by the lack of regular contact. It's not that you cherish them any less but others come along to compete for time. Also, there was a gnawing sense that such responsibility-free existence couldn't last for ever.

In the meantime we made the most of what remained. We regularly hung around the Railway Tavern.

You know the story of the young boy growing up in the fifties, fed on a diet of Richard Todd and Audie Murphy war movies, asking his father, 'What did you do in the war, Daddy?' Expecting tales of heroism, he heard instead that he was store-keeper. I lived through a momentous half-century; the Berlin wall went up and it came down, communism was deified and discredited and so on. This year was a watershed in the story of cricket. Peter Oborne's excellent biography *D'Oliveira* explores the actions of men whose lot it was to shape history. A mixture of deviousness and well-meaning but misguided individuals, tried to say that more good would come out of continuing with the planned tour of South Africa than by cancelling it. I must confess that I was in that camp. At the heart of the conflict was whether South Africa would permit D'Oliveira to tour if selected. D'Oliveira's form was patchy and he was dropped from the side playing Australia. Then Roger Prideaux pulled out of the squad for the Oval Test and D'Oliveira was brought back. Ever the man for the big occasion, he responded with a magnificent 158. On the last day, rain threatened to deny England a win and we expected a draw. We went to the Railway Tavern, now the proud owner of a colour television set. There we saw Cowdrey supervising the mopping up operation. We saw D'Oliveira make the crucial breakthrough and Underwood then run through the Australian batting line up and win the match with only a minute or two to spare.

More fun and games followed, D'Oliveira was not included in the touring party. Then Cartwright pulled out and D'Oliveira was in. South Africa's Prime Minister B. J. Voster said he was not welcome and the tour was cancelled.

I'm not proud of the stance I took but I don't intend to air-brush my character.

Clowning on the last day in Croydon. Eric McGill and Peter Wilson doing the Atlas bit, Mike Woodburn, Dave Smissen, Geoff & Christine Jackson. Allen was camera-shy and Kevin had gone a.w.o.l

Eventually, the move to 66 Cheapside happened. That building couldn't cope with the additional influx. Within the Actuarial Department, the Northern had detailed and documented guidelines, whereas CU appeared to have none. CU was also actively following a graduate recruitment policy and most of the post 1966 intake was from Oxbridge and brighter than me.

Kevin left to join International Life, an aggressive new US life company based in Wembley. Mashuque left to join Abbey Life. Dave Reynolds left to join a firm of consulting actuaries and by the end of the year I'd agreed to join International Life starting the following February. My salary leapt from around £1,000 (I can't remember the amount) to £1,850.

After the CU takeover, the social clubs were merged. One day the Chess Club was short of a player in the first team in a game that evening against Noble Lowndes. Urgent requests were sent in those pre-email days. Having nothing better to do, I said I'd play, but warned that I was hopeless and usually played in the fourth team. They put that down to modesty and put me down on Board 1 (of the first team). There are six players in a team and the best should be on Board 1 and the worst on Board 6. Adherence to that convention ensured that everyone had a good game. I suspect our captain was cheating and offering me up as sacrifice.

Well what had to happen, happened. We started at a quarter to six and by six I'd lost my queen, both knights and a rook and my defence had been smashed. Chess etiquette demanded that I should resign. But there was no way that I, on Board 1, was going to resign that early. It would be humiliating. So I lived move by move with no strategy other than to survive. My opponent, a serious chess thinker was visibly annoyed that I didn't resign. He also looked for deep motivation in my moves when there was none there. He started making mistakes and eventually at around seven, I checkmated him. He was not a happy bunny and kept muttering under his breath, 'No manners, should have resigned.'

It was the most satisfying win of my life.

6. 1969

I was recruited by International Life in the expectation that I would qualify as an actuary after the summer exams. In the event I failed both the remaining subjects, again. No one said anything. It was surreal. From my perspective, I joined them on the rebound from the commercialism of CU, a case of 'out of the frying pan into the fire.' The contrast with the Northern was total. At the Northern you always felt that you were providing a service. There were certain products we weren't competitive in and if a broker asked for a quote, we'd give it but always add a disclaimer. 'You should shop around as you may be able to get better terms elsewhere.' International Life dealt exclusively through a direct sales force. Although the sales mantra was that they cut out the middleman, the products were expensive. We used to joke that our motto was 'Never knowingly oversold'. I joined in the newly formed Pensions Department where we dealt with corporations and value for money was important. Not surprisingly we never made a success of it.

I didn't fully understand their sales process until I joined them. It was what we call pyramid selling. In each sales branch there is a large sales force with a hierarchy of senior salesmen, assistant branch manager and branch manager above them. Each branch is part of a region with a regional sales manager and above all the regional sales managers is the national sales manager. The salesman at the lowest rung may get commission of say 30% on each new sale. His direct boss may make 10% on the same sale; the next person up 5%, the next 2.5% and so an. The national sales manager gets perhaps ½ % on every sale. Thus every salesman is motivated to be promoted to the next rung up so that in addition to full commission on his own sales he gets an override on every sale made by salesmen under him.

This is standard pyramid selling. What gave this company tremendous momentum was that all salesmen and also senior admin staff got shares in the parent company. At the time I joined, the share price was doubling in value every eighteen months. I remember people doing projections: 'doubles in eighteen months, quadruples in three years; sixteen times in six years, 256 times in twelve years. My shares are worth £4,000 today; I'd be a millionaire in twelve years; a dozen years of graft and I can retire.' I did the sums for some of them and remember asking if it was credible to expect to double every eighteen months; once, twice or even thrice, yes, but for ever? But I was ignored for being 'a typical actuary'. The motivation this gave was tremendous. There was a buzz about the place that was infectious. To me it was like leaving a monastry and entering a brothel. I couldn't get my brain round it. Actually that's a terrible analogy but I'm struggling to find a suitable one. Let's put it this way, it was a real eye-opener.

Not long afterwards, we went to a sales convention at the Royal Albert Hall. A fancy car was on display as the top prize. Draped across it were a couple of nubile girls clad in top and trousers made of netting and nothing else as far as I could make out from a distance. There were a couple of warm-up men preparing the audience, correction, whipping up the audience, for the arrival of the founder of IOS, the parent company.

'Bernie is coming, Bernie is coming, he's been held up,' and so on. Eventually he did arrive. Amid great fanfare and swooning there appeared a small man, not much bigger than me, with a two-day stubble, which in those days was regarded as unkempt, little hair on the top, a girl on each arm. I thought momentarily that I'd strayed into the Playboy Club. A mike was brought to him and lowered to his height.

'Welcome fellow missionaries,' he said and we had perhaps five minutes of sustained applause for that profound statement. I'd never seen anything like it.

In the summer I had to give a talk to the sales force on pensions and annuities, being the products I'd been involved in designing. I'd never given a talk in public and I was reluctant to make a fool of myself, but I had to do it. So off I went to Leeds the night before and practised in my hotel room. The next morning I gave the talk. It was about the nuts and bolts of the product, nothing about why someone might want them or about how to sell them. When I finished, everyone cheered wildly and for long. I was taken aback as I didn't think it was that good, just OK but it was reassuring all the same to hear the applause. During the coffee break, a young Asian salesman cornered me and said politely, 'That was a very good talk.'

I thanked him whereupon, in a low voice he said to me. 'Mr Iqbal, can you tell me what an annuity really is?'

I was flabbergasted. 'But, but you just said it was a very good talk. Everyone clapped and you clapped too. Didn't you understand it?'

'Mr Iqbal, I clapped because everyone else clapped. I didn't understand a word you said.'

That deflated me and I made further soundings. I had to know whether he was dense or my talk was dense. It turned out that all salesmen were trained to be positive and to cheer and clap every speaker regardless of content. I bet if I'd stood up and said, 'Guys, all your mothers are dead,' they'd still have cheered me.

I had further evidence of a salesman's psyche when I joined them in the bar that lunchtime. One salesman, Norman, said to another, pointing to a particularly attractive young barmaid; well, a barmaid with a particularly attractive top half. The rest of her was obscured by the bar, 'Hey Ted, Look at that crumpet behind the bar. Isn't she gorgeous?'

'Phwow! Not half.'

'Bet you can't bed her tonight.'

'Of course I can. Every girl has her price. Beats working behind the bar.'

'OK, let's see you do it?'

'It's a piece of cake. Set me a difficult challenge.'

Another salesman, Ian joined in and said, 'No, I've tried that last night. She's as tight as a barnacle. I'll give you a difficult challenge. See if she will accept £20 from you.'

'In return for what?' asked Ted.

'Nothing. See if she'll accept a gift of £20.'

Ted glanced at the barmaid again and their eyes met. She sensed that they were talking about her.

'What's in it for me?' asked Ted.

'I'll replace the £20 and buy you a pint.'

'Right, you're on.' Ted combed his hair, straightened his tie, took two ten pound notes from his wallet and went up to the barmaid and waited.

'What would you like?' she asked.

'I'd like to give you this,' he said handing her the notes.

'What do you want?'

'Nothing. I just want to give you this money.'

'But what do you want? We do drinks and we do food. What do you want? Twenty quid is a lot of money.'

'No, no, it's just by way of thanks.'

'Thanks for what?'

'For being here.'

'I'm not sure I like you or your friends. Is this some sort of game?'

'How can I convince you that I'm merely thanking you for being here?'

'You can't buy me you know. Take your filthy money back.'

As Ted returned beaten, Ian and Norman burst out laughing.

I returned home thinking that I'd better get trained in public speaking. Others must have reached a similar conclusion as Personnel Department phoned me to say that I'd been selected to go on a training course on public speaking. There were six of us and we were taught the right approach and were asked to prepare a talk for the final day.

I decided to lampoon pyramid selling. The talk is given to the sales force by its national sales manager. The company makes jockstraps and I made much play of the company's motto, 'We're here to give you support'. Several other jokes were thrown in. When I gave the talk people started laughing, at first slowly then uncontrollably. That was the intended outcome but I lost my nerve completely. I couldn't work out whether they were laughing with me or at me. By the end everyone was rolling on the floor and I was a complete wreck, shot to pieces.

I did become a good public speaker, but only after the several years it took me to get over that disaster. Part of my problem was that lacking physical and vocal presence, self confidence was fragile. Public speaking is all about self confidence. When you have a hundred people sat in front of you, all attentive, if you're not confident you're overcome with a deep sense of humility. You wonder what it is that you have that would be worth their while. What you need to convince yourself is that in one tiny component of the universe of knowledge you know just a bit more than the audience and that's what they've come to listen.

Actors must fight this all the time. I remember seeing a matinée performance of an Alan Ayckbourn comedy in which Felicity Kendal starred. The play was littered with one-liners and she delivered them with superb timing but provoked absolutely no reaction from the audience. I really felt for her.

I started playing cricket again by joining International Life's team. I remember going to a sports shop to buy my own bat, pads and gloves as those provided by the team would be too large; and for hygienic reasons, my own box, my first box and, as it happened, my last box. It was made of hard plastic and cost 5/6d. I know that for a fact as the price label was still on it two, no three, decades later. Trousers presented a great problem. As the shop salesman said in a Jeevesian style put-down: 'The trouble with you, Sir, is that you have the waist of an adult but the inside leg of a boy.'

'Are you telling me that I'm short and fat?' I asked him.

'I didn't say that, Sir.'

The International Life's team had a couple of handy players. The rest were mediocre. I presented myself as a bowler and so was put in at number eleven. My phantom finger had gone but spinning the ball was difficult so I lengthened my run-up and bowled gentle medium pace; in theory. In practice, I can't recall ever being asked to bowl. So, it was back to my sub-teenage years; I was there to make up numbers. The truth is that Martin Johnson's immortal phrase, 'can't bat, can't bowl, can't field' must surely have been coined with me in mind.

We played teams like Ealing College, Hayes and Harlington and London Transport 2nd XI. Ealing College had a West Indian coach, a giant, built like Charlie Griffith. He opened the bowling off a long run up. Our opening batsman, whose name I shall not reveal, saw this imposing figure and self-preservation instincts took over. He hastily backed away. From near the square leg umpire, he saw to his consternation the bowler delivering the gentlest of balls, which barely got to the other end. Unfortunately it was dead straight and clean bowled him before he could get back. In the bar we teased him, 'Fancy being scared of a slow medium pacer.'

'Nobody told me he was that slow.'

'The wicket keeper standing up was a clue.'

'I didn't see that. All I saw was this big black fella bearing down on me, like a sooty steam engine locomotive. I decided to get the hell out of there.'

When we played the London Transport 2nd XI, we were quite confident as we rattled up two hundred odd in our allotted overs (30, I think). LT2XI got them in ten. A young guy who played for Barbados second team, murdered us.

Imran Khan in his various autobiographies and biographies made a great virtue out of his abstemiousness and said he always drank milk instead. Well, although by 1969 I was regularly drinking cider, in the pavilion after play was over, I used to drink a pint of milk. The use of the past tense is appropriate because I didn't do it for long as it made me burp.

A collector's item, the only recorded photograph of me as a batsman in my favourite position, that of non-striker. ILI v. Tokyngton, June 1969

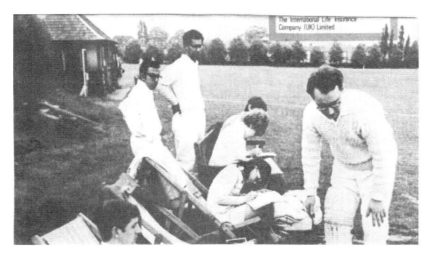

Same match, Kevin and I, behind the deck chairs, wait our turn to bat.

Late in August, the Northern gang had one last reunion. Eric came down from Scotland specifically for it. We had planned to meet in the Railway Tavern and walk to Brighton from there. We met and reminisced as if we were a bunch of pensioners who hadn't met for ages, rather than a few months. Eric, Allen, Mashuque and Kevin were there and so was Peter Wilson. We had a few drinks and something to eat. We forgot all about the walk until at about 9.30 Mike Woodburn turned up, in full athletic gear, asking when we were going to start. No-one wanted to be the one to admit that they didn't really want to do it, so at midnight five of us (me, Allen, Mike, his then girlfriend and Eric) set off from the Railway Tavern. Kevin acted as a a guide-cum-scout and followed us an hour later in his car. I gave up at about Redhill where Kevin picked me up. I hid in his backseat not wanting to admit that I had given up before the girl.

Mike and Allen eventually got to Brighton and claimed the world record for walking drunk, in office clothes in the rain for over eleven hours. The next day, having not slept and probably none too fresh, we had been invited to tea at the Jacksons' house, the very Jackson who used to hold Friday evening concerts in Mashuque's room. I doubt we were the best of company

West Indies and New Zealand were the touring teams and I saw neither. West Indies were in transition, the great team of the early sixties breaking up and the stars of the late seventies not yet on the scene. Their bowling was particularly weak and Sobers was tired. New Zealand had a Hanif clone in Glenn Turner.

The most influential event was the end of Tom Graveney's Test career. He played in a one-day game on the Sunday rest day in a Test. He was asked not to. So it was a straight choice between forgoing his Test career and forgoing the fee for the one-day match. The latter, at £1,000, won. So ended the career of one of the most elegant batsmen I've seen; a most unEnglish player because he was a front-foot player. As he was the designated captain in Cowdrey's absence, his departure paved the way for Illingworth.

Although I didn't see any of the Tests, I did go to a number of county and Sunday league matches, usually at the Oval, but I was also following

Glamorgan closely. Majid was in great form. I went to see their match against Worcestershire at Cardiff. On a turning pitch with Gifford in great form, he scored a scarcely credible 156 out of 265. The next best score was Alan Jones's 39. Tom Graveney in his autobiography said that he was teaching the English how to bat under English conditions. I must have died a hundred deaths watching him. He kept dancing down the pitch to Gifford and Slade and I kept thinking 'he cannot possibly get there,' but he always did. He won the match for Glamorgan and with it the championship.

During Wimbledon, there was an amazing first round match between Pancho Gonzales and Charlie Pasarell which was spread over two days. Tie-breaks hadn't been introduced and the first set went to 22–24 to Pasarell. In the end Gonzales won 22–24, 1–6, 16–14, 6–3, 11–9. My recollection is that he was so knackered that he lost in the next round. In fact, he somehow got through the next two rounds before Arthur Ashe knocked him out. He was 41.

I watched a fair amount of football considering that it wasn't my sport. Mostly I watched with Allan although I watched the occasional West Ham or Crystal Palace match with Dave Reynolds. I can't recall which year I saw some of the matches so I'll just put down general recollections. I remember going to a midweek Spurs-Chelsea match at Stamford Bridge. A dull scrappy match it was, with frequent fouls and hold-ups. Spurs won by a single goal, a typically opportunistic one by Greaves, completely against the run of play. A tall guy standing in front of me blocked my view and I missed the goal altogether. I thought I'd catch it on the replay, forgetting that I wasn't sitting at home. I dashed back home to catch it on BBC1 at 10.40 and you know what? I didn't recognise the match as the one that I'd just watched. Ninety scrappy minutes had been reduced to twenty minutes of fluid and exciting football.

As the year drew to a close, little did I know that this was the beginning of the end of an era. The joke is that if you remember the sixties you weren't there. Well, I remember every tiny detail of that period and I was there. I didn't do sex and drugs but it was a memorable age nonetheless.

7. 1970

I really must see a shrink one day. My intellectual inconsistencies are surely worth psychoanalysis. Peter Hain was waging a campaign to stop the planned South African tour of England. As my political leanings were increasingly left-wing at the time I should have supported him. Instead, 'keep politics out of sport', was my mantra when clearly the South African Government was making it central to it. The truth was that the Springboks were the best team in the world and I desperately wanted to see Peter and Graeme Pollock, Barry Richards, Mike Proctor and Eddie Barlow. The tour was eventually called off and a five Test series of England *v.* The Rest of the World was drawn up. A squad was picked for the latter from foreign players playing county cricket plus a few South African stars: Barry Richards, Eddie Barlow, Graeme Pollock, Rohan Kanhai, Clive Lloyd, Garry Sobers (captain), Mushtaq Mohammed, Farook Engineer, Mike Proctor, Intikhab Alam, Garth McKenzie, Peter Pollock, Lance Gibbs and Derek Murray.

I watched quite a few days of the Lord's Test and the Saturdays of the other four Tests. Although England lost the series 4–1, in reality it was much closer than that. Illingworth was a canny captain. Even when his bowlers were being taken apart he had a smile on his face as if everything was going according to plan, his plan. I sensed that the English players were playing for their country whereas no such motivation existed for the ROTW team's players. They were playing for their pride.

Mind you, nothing could dim the brilliance of Sobers. He topped the batting with the most runs at the highest average, took the most wickets and came second in the bowling averages. Neither Barry Richards nor Graeme Pollock did themselves justice, Graeme waiting until the last Test to shine. Eddie Barlow and. Proctor were the two South African who consistently shone. Running in at lightning speed and delivering off the wrong foot, Proctor dismissed Alan Jones on debut for a five and zero in the first Test and Brian Luckhurst for a pair in the last. Luckily, Brian had some good scores in earlier Tests in the series but Jones's career as Test player did not survive that failure. In fact even his failure went unrecorded as the series was stripped of Test status subsequently. It seemed a bit harsh, as the runs scored and wickets taken during the series were more precious than all the runs Barrington and Parfitt scored against weak Pakistan, New Zealand and Indian teams.

The Lord's Test was a one man show. Sobers, coming on as first change after McKenzie and Proctor, skittled out England for 127, taking six wickets for twenty-one and then he scored a fabulous 183, combining watertight defence with aggressive run-making. In England's second innings he gave Intikhab a marathon spell and the leg-spinner responded with six wickets. England won the next Test but lost the following three.

Kevin and I went to the Birmingham, Nottingham and Leeds Tests to see each Saturday's play. He had a Morris 1100 and used to drive from Croydon to Cricklewood to pick me up and then we went from there. When we went to Birmingham we had to park the car in a designated field. A West Indian who parked alongside us befriended us and followed us into the ground. We couldn't get rid of him. He didn't speak much, but whenever he did he spoke in epigrams and homilies that were given with a finality that brooked no argument or discussion. Most of his tirade was against the white man and what they'd done to the black people and why we should avoid them. 'I wouldn't even piss on them; it's a waste of waste,' seemed mildly funny. As to white women, 'they're not worth it. I wouldn't f**k them for fear of contaminating my c**k.' He kept this up throughout the day. When play ended for the day and we were walking back to our cars, he said, 'I'd better go and freshen myself, I've got a date.'

'A black girl, I presume?' I asked rhetorically,

'No, white,' he said with a smile. The diatribe at the ground was for our benefit. He didn't practice what he preached.

When we went to Leeds we arrived late. I don't remember much of the match other than the sight of Don Wilson. When play ended, we decided to go to Scarborough and spend the night there and see the sights on the following day, Sunday. We had a fish and chips supper before setting off. We didn't have a detailed map and got lost. Late in the evening we pulled up in a lay-by and slept in the car. It was surprisingly cool. When we woke up late morning on Sunday, we decided to give Scarborough a miss and drove down south. When we got to Derby we went to the county ground to watch, for a couple of hours, Surrey playing a Sunday league match. We then set off home.

One day at work my boss said to me, 'Icki, I'd like you to meet someone,' pointing to a person standing next to him. A slightly built man, not much taller than me, perhaps five feet five or six, with warm eyes and lips ready to burst into smile, no hair and a face and forehead covered in red veins like someone in love with alcohol. As his smile became more expansive I though to myself, 'It can't be, it can't be, Oh my God it is.' It was Bill Edrich. We exchanged a few words. I was too starstruck to say much and I deeply regretted not getting notice of the meeting. He was a thoroughly unassuming guy and there were a thousand things I ought to have asked him. 'What was it like to face Lindwall in his prime? What was the truth behind your omission from the 1950/51 tour of Australia. What was the Indian tour under Lord Tennyson in 1937 like?' But I was tongue-tied and star-struck. Bill was a direct salesman for International Life but, alas, not for long, as he joined a competitor. A couple of years ago I read Alan Hill's biography of Bill. Apparently he didn't drink much but he didn't need to. He had a very low threshold of alcohol tolerance. He was like Keith Miller, having cheated death many times during the War, both lived for today as if there would be no tomorrow.

Actually, even if I had got notice of meeting Bill, I doubt if I would have asked him more searching questions. To me sporting heroes were for deification, to be kept on a pedestal. If you get too close to them they may turn out to be mortals with flaws. That would never do.

I must mention one colleague at International Life, who had a profound influence on shaping my character. He joined the firm in 1970. We were both at the same stage in our exams but he passed his remaining subject that year whereas I didn't. So he ended up being my boss. A gregarious and extroverted character, John Porter gradually drew me out of my shell and coarsened my language. In a reversal of the reformed sinner syndrome, I probably went too far the other way. Looking back, before John arrived on the scene I must have been insufferably nice. No wonder Mashuque hated me when he was drunk.

John lived in Epping, a long way away from Wembley where our office was. One weekend I went to his house and from there went to

Harlow to see Essex play Cambridge University, for whom Majid Khan was playing. He played one exquisite on drive for four and then snicked one to the wicket keeper. The undergraduates struggled on, only Dudley Owen-Thomas getting any runs. When Essex batted, Keith Fletcher, the rising English star sent us to sleep. One of John's stories that I remember was that the girl friend of one of his friends used to boast that she had bedded Colin Milburn, Mushtaq Mohammed and Denis Law; three sportsman who had nothing in common other than being a sportsman. She must have been a non-discriminating groupie.

International Life was a slick sales operation which would have risen to greater heights were it not for the fact that some of the people at the very top were, shall we say, not quite kosher. Its parent company, IOS, was founded to sell mutual funds door to door, initially to US forces living in Europe. In the UK, the Prevention of Frauds Investment Act 1958 prevented the sale of unit trusts (our equivalent of mutual funds) door to door. So they set up a life insurance company to do much the same thing. All the sales force were part of a sister company and the life company's monies were quite safe. All of the salesmen and management had visions of unimaginable wealth from their share options. However, once discrepancies and dishonesties surfaced, confidence evaporated and the shares became unsaleable as no one could put a reliable price on them. By a curious coincidence, its auditors were Arthur Andersen, who thirty years later would be the auditors of Enron.

The UK life insurance company, which was financially sound, lost its salesmen and we went though a quiet period. With time to spare and sorrows to drown, the pub became a regular refuge. Friday evenings were spent in the Century pub. John was the self-appointed buyer of rounds, using the kitty. That meant that everyone had to drink at his speed. He could down as many as twelve pints in an evening whereas my limit was two or three pints of cider He still kept buying me rounds so that come half past ten there could be perhaps nine or ten undrunk glasses of cider on the table.

One day someone mixed vodka in my cider. That was the only time in my life that I've passed out and someone had to take me home.

England's soccer team went to Mexico to defend its title. Allen's father owned an electrical goods shop. He invited us to watch the opening match in his house on colour TV, his parents being away. Owing to the time difference we watched it late at night. It was England's opening match against Mexico and was a turgid 0–0 draw. The colour control on the television was unsteady and from time to time the Mexican's colour, which was red or brown would change to white, England's colour, causing us confusion. Also, the vertical control was not functioning properly so that all players looked stunted. We had a good side and should have got to the final but, when leading 2–0 against Germany, Bobby Charlton was substituted to save him for the semi-final. Uwe Seeler stole two goals and Muller another. It was nothing less than a heist.

At least that is how I remember it. I checked it out and found that the reality was slightly different. England did get two goals but in the 68th minute Beckenbauer pulled one back. It was after that, a minute after that, when England were only 2–1 up that Ramsey substituted Bobby Charlton, to save him for the semi as he was tiring in the altitude. It was then that Seeler equalised, some would say he didn't; the ball hit his head and went in. In extra time a Hurst goal was disallowed and Muller scored the winning goal. I have always prided myself on my memory for useless facts and I couldn't believe that I'd got the detail of such a memorable match wrong. I mentioned this to two friends with similarly good memories, Steve Shurety and John Porter. Both of them thought that England were 2–0 up when Bobby Charlton was substituted. Whilst Steve was prepared to accept that he might be wrong if I had checked out the facts, John thought that Wikipedia must have got it wrong. Perhaps he is right.

Germany lost to Italy in the semis. The final was between Brazil and Italy and Brazil won 4–1 with goals by Pele, Gerson, Jairzinho and Carlos Alberto. Brazil dominated the tournament and a victory was their fair due. Pele was outstanding but they had other players too, not least the bow-legged Jairzinho. Had England got to the final I'd have fancied their chances. Brazil had no defence whilst England did.

Little did we know that it would be a few world cups before we would better the 1970 performance.

In the winter of 1970/71 Illingworth led a successful campaign to win back the Ashes. There were a number of analogies with Strauss's campaign in 2010/11. Australia had returned from a punishing tour (India and South Africa, I ask you). Its bowling was weak, the spearhead Garth McKenzie being a spent force. Its captain Bill Lawry was replaced by Ian Chappell for the last Test. Fast bowling undid them, although it was speed and hostility rather than swing. England had a young beanpole of a fast bowler (Willis instead of Finn). Like Strauss, Illingworth had a definite plan that he executed brilliantly. Both had a united team (although Cowdrey did not buy into it). Snow and Boycott were on the form of their lives (as were Anderson and Cook). Knott had an outstanding tour (as did Prior). The one difference of substance was that there was no Andy Flower. Dave Clark, the manager was not an Illingworth devotee. But it did not matter, as Illingworth was not one to share leadership. As captain, he would no more share responsibility with his manager than, a quarter of a century later, as manager he would share it with Mike Atherton, the skipper.

I have two outstanding memories of the tour. One was Illingworth winning the last Test by a mixture of guile and skill when he had little to play with. The other was Boycott's bat-throwing incident when given run out. He refused to walk. Years later he was shown a slow-motion replay and asked, 'Surely that shows you were clearly out?'

'Of course I was out, I know that. But the umpire couldn't have been sure and should have given me the benefit of the doubt.'

Lawry was summarily sacked as skipper for the final Test and Ian Chappell installed as the new skipper. The heartless way in which this was done had a profound impact upon Ian. He was to prove an inspirational captain but he swore that nobody would ever sack him and resigned his leadership when he had a few years still in him.

Ian has written caustically about Bradman after he'd gone from this world. David Frith in his *Bodyline Autopsy* concluded that it was Bradman who'd leaked Woodfull's statement ('There's two teams out there, only one of them is playing cricket') and let Fingleton take the wrap. There's a book waiting to be written focusing on the flip side of this Australian deity.

In October of 1970 I went to India on holiday and married Kadeeja. I had kept it quiet, but Kevin got wind of it and very nearly got a party ready to greet me as I arrived at Heathrow.

Thank God, he didn't.

The following year, on the 25th June she joined me in England; the very day I qualified as an actuary. I threw a party for my friends.

8. 1971–72.

The sixties was a tremendous decade for me personally; carefree, happy, full of novel experiences. It was replaced by an altogether different decade. I changed and the world around me changed. I got married; we bought a house and started a family. After I qualified as an actuary I began to achieve positions of responsibility and work started to encroach on leisure time. I had treated the sixties as an extended period of fun with no care or responsibilities. Soon double digit inflation would change the economic and employment landscape, the entire world would change completely. Caution and cynicism would replace optimism. It has to be said that I wasn't the finished article and was caught unprepared. Cricket took a back seat. I still followed it as avidly as before but now it was through the media; John Woodcock, John Arlott, Richie Benaud and Jim Laker.

All these things are obvious in hindsight, but the changes crept gradually up on me. The years 1971 and 1972 were those of transition. We didn't know that we were saying *Good bye, Yellow Brick Road*.

Followers of Pakistan's cricket team had to deal with a new set of emotions. In the fifties we grew up with reasonable prospects of success. We had a team of carnivorous lions, unlike the meek vegetarians from India. Even when they were beaten, our team would go down fighting, they would not capitulate like the Indians in 1952 and 1959. The 1962 tour of England changed our perceptions: we were just as abject as the Indians; cut from the same cloth, peas from the same pod, all the clichés you'd find in a bad novel. So we fans adapted to that. We knew our new place in the world, we were the whipping boys. Even Peter Parfitt filled his boots with centuries against our bowling and Len Coldwell, journeyman medium-pacer from Worcester, took a five-for against our batting. We accepted it on the basis that someone had to come last. We drew comfort from heroic but futile pursuit of lost causes, such as Asif Iqbal's 146 at the Oval in 1967. But by the early seventies we had some high quality cricketers, Majid Khan, Asif Iqbal, Mushtaq Mohammed, Zaheer Abbas, Wasim Bari. We dared to dream of success. Alas, during the first half of the decade on countless occasions fate seduced us with the prospect of victory, only to take it away from us. It was a horrible feeling. I don't mind being thrashed by an innings and 579 runs, as Australia were by England in 1938, or even losing by an innings after conceding a first innings lead of only 46, as New Zealand, all out 26, submitted to England in 1955. But it is devastating to lose by 25 runs chasing 231 after being at one stage 184 for 5; or losing by one wicket when the opponent at one stage were 64 behind with one wicket left, or being all out for 83 chasing 158. Take it from me, the ache of despair is more enduring than the joy of success. But if the fans suffered, what about the players? Fear of failure was barring their path to success. The term 'choking' hadn't yet been coined, but that was what was happening to the players. It was a psychological barrier. Our combativeness improved by the end of the seventies but the capacity for self-destruction remained. For the next forty years, when the team had a succession of world-class cricketers and some all-time greats, I was never able to savour success because of the fear that there would be an unexpected twist. The most recent example of that was at Lord's when Mohammed Amir had a sensational spell, making English batsmen look like novices, only to be followed by the great Trott–Broad stand, which as it turned out was just the apéritif to the devil's supper. That is why we never suspected match-fixing as we were used to inexplicable collapses.

A question that has never been satisfactorily answered, or if it has been then I haven't seen it, is: Why does a person become a sports fan? Is there a defining gene and does it transcend race, generations and sport? I'm not a psychologist but I've speculated on it.

The first clue is the fact that the word fan is short for fanatic. The allegiance is blinkered, possibly blind. Why else would you stay loyal through thick and thin, through changes in playing style, your personal circumstance or team's circumstance? Few marriages are that strong. Even political loyalty is not that strong. An Englishman who emigrates to the US or Australia will, after a while, shift his political allegiance to align it to his economic interests. He'd still continue to support Tottenham at football and England at cricket. Perhaps it is a metaphor for some part of your personality that is constant and unchanging; sport can fulfil that role because in truth it does not matter; we only think that it does. Bill Shankly was utterly wrong when he said, 'Football is not a matter of life and death; its much more than that.' It's precisely because it is NOT a matter of life and death that we surrender ourselves uncritically to it. That is why poorer communities are more devoted to sport than affluent ones. That is why most fans are male, as men try to seek refuge from responsibilities whilst women face up to theirs.

All this might be pure hokum but that is my hypothesis. It might be true in my case. Kadeeja always says that I don't take my responsibilities seriously.

These thoughts were far from my mind on Valentine's Day in 1971, the day currency decimalisation was introduced in Britain. India and Pakistan had done that in the fifties and done it overnight. In Britain it was after years of planning. I'm told that it was a major logistic operation for banks and supermarkets because the tills had to be loaded with sufficient new coins. For me and my actuarial colleagues it was a sad day. We number crunchers had lost a skill. You see, on the calculator all answers were in decimals anyway and we knew how to convert them into pounds shillings and pence to the nearest pence. We knew that .00416667 was a penny and .00208333 was ha'penny and we knew the decimal equivalent of every amount under a pound. We could round to the nearest penny in our head. The new currency made such old skills redundant. A decade later I had much sympathy for printers when Murdoch moved production to Wapping and introduced computer-aided typesetting.

As I mentioned in the previous chapter, I qualified as an actuary on 25th June, the day Kadeeja arrived in England. Inflation was raising its ugly head and completely distorting everything. My salary had gone up from £2,100 to £2,400, a 14% rise in recognition of becoming an actuary. I was naturally thrilled. But blow me, a month later there was a 'cost of living correction' which gave a whopping 25% increase. My salary rose to £3,000 without my doing anything.

Naseem moved out of the room we shared into another room so that Kadeeja could move in. Out went the bunk beds and in came a double bed. I also rented the room next door and used it as a kitchen.

In the autumn Naseem married Jill in Lowestoft. His father did not take kindly to his son marrying a Christian and I had to act as the go-between. In the end he had to give in, partly because he could not stop it and partly because he'd done the same thing himself.

One day in September I sneaked off to the Oval. Surrey were playing Glamorgan and, if they beat them, they'd win the championship for the first time since 1958. It was the third day and the game was nicely poised. In the end Glamorgan were set 287 in five hours to win and they went for it. The ball was seaming and swinging and Geoff Arnold was a handful. Roy Fredericks and Majid Khan had a good stand before Roy was out. Majid carried on. It was a marvellous innings, watchful, but never missing scoring opportunities. By late afternoon it was quite dark and eventually Majid snicked Arnold to slips. Glamorgan then shut up shop and saw off the rest of the day, just; they were down to the last man. There were angry scenes at the end with the Surrey supporters heckling Tony Lewis and Peter Walker.

Not long after that we started house hunting. A typical three bedroom house was costing around £9,000, prices having risen sharply. They kept rising as we looked. Not having a car and not having narrowed down the area to live in, it took us a while. In the end we made an offer of £11,250 which was accepted. A month later he wanted another £500. With the anger of the naïve, I said, 'We agreed on a deal. You can't go back on your word.'

'Take it or leave it.'

Like a fool I left it. Six months later I moved into an identical house for which I paid £13,750. There's a Hindi song which goes:

> 'Sub kuch seekha hamnay na seekhi hoshiari
> Such hai duniya waalo ke ham hain anari'

Which would translate as

> 'Of knowledge I have plenty, but streetwise I'm not
> Of the ways of the world I do not know a jot'

Pakistan toured in the early part of the summer. It was the strongest batting line-up they had sent until then, even without Majid, who was at Cambridge. The team was one or two bowlers short of Test class. That is why they couldn't force a win in the first Test. In the third Test, paradoxically, the bowlers set up a winning position, leaving Pakistan to get 231 to win. After early failures, Asif Iqbal and Sadiq Mohammed got together in a highly responsible stand, but they were out-thought by Illingworth. Brearley might have been the best at reading people's minds but no-one could beat Illingworth on creating fear and uncertainty in the opposition's minds.

This was Imran's first tour as a green eighteen-year-old. He was a peripheral figure. In his autobiography, he referred to an official dinner at which the team's manager expressed gratitude to the British for 'teaching us how to use knife and fork'. Imran was extremely embarrassed by this act of apparent sycophancy. Pakistanis don't do irony, so it would not have occurred to Imran that it was a tongue-in-cheek comment.

India toured in the second half of 1971 having had a successful tour of West Indies and having discovered an all-time great in Sunil Gavaskar. They had a great spin quartet and were ably led, not by Pataudi but by Ajit Wadekar. England were caught unprepared in the first Test which they could have lost. There was the famous incident of John Snow barging Sunil Gavaskar. For some reason my standout memory is of Abid Ali the opening bowler. He had a run up as long as Wes Hall's. He ambled in rocking from one side to the next, with no acceleration and then delivered the ball at a slower speed than he ran in. I'm sure that if he ever delivered a wide he could run after it and retrieve the ball before it reached the batsman. It staggers me that he had a six-wicket haul in a Test match. In the third Test at the Oval, India won for the first time in England. Bhagwat Chandrasekhar set it up with a 6 for 38 haul but they still had to get 170-odd against Illingworth's mind games. That they got there was largely due to Dilip Sardesai.

John Player Sunday League brought more cricket to our lounges. It was a pleasure to listen to John Arlott's commentary accompanying the visuals. He had such a vivid turn of phrase and a dry sense of humour. He was a master of the understatement, the very antithesis of Mark Nicholas. I remember a match in which Somerset were in the field. He was describing the field setting and he said something like 'And standing at fine leg is the new signing, Joel Garner. You can easily recognise him; he's the only one wearing a half-sleeve shirt.' I mean, you'd have thought that a guy who was six foot eight and jet black was pretty recognisable. Or his broadcast of Bradman's last test innings at the Oval in 1948 – no I wasn't there, but BBC issued an LP celebrating 21 years of outside broadcast on BBC Sport (which included a famous boat race when John Snagge said, 'It's close, very close, I can't say who's won it; its either Oxford or Cambridge'). John Arlott said, 'Hollies bowls and Bradman plays it in the direction of the Houses of Parliament. It doesn't get that far as mid-off intercepts it. Hollies bowls again and he's bowled, Bradman's bowled.'

There's a story about Arthur Morris, the great Australian left-hander, who was in a bar in England when he heard someone talk about Bradman.

'Jees, do you know, he averaged nearly hundred in Tests? In fact he needed only four runs in his last Test innings and, blow me, guess what he got? A duck, I ask you.'

'That's right,' said Arthur.

He turned to Arthur and asked, 'You knew about Bradman's duck?'

'I was there.'

'You're kidding aren't you?'

'No.'

'OK, what were you doing?'

'I was at the other end.'

'I don't believe it. What's your name?'

'Arthur Morris.'

'How many did you get?'

'196.'

What cruel fate. A man scores 196 and wins the Test match for his country (with a little help from Lindwall) and all that people can remember is another bloke's duck.

Richie Benaud has built up an enormous reputation as a pithy but straight-laced television commentator. But there are two other sides to him that are worth noting. Shujauddin, who had a long stand with Saeed Ahmed in a Test match against Australia in 1959/60 said to me that Benaud and his team responded to his dead bat defence with coarse sledging. The other point about Richie is that coarse humour appealed to him. I can't resist two stories he relates in his autobiography. The first is about Alan Ross, a poet turned cricket correspondent who wrote *Australia 55*, perhaps the best tour book ever, covering the Tyson tour.

He was commentating on a New Zealand *v.* England Test when the opening bowler, Bob Cunis, was bowling medium-paced filth. Alan said, 'His bowling is like his name, neither one thing nor the other.'

The second concerns Keith Miller whom he idolised. Richie reckoned that he was the best (Aussie) captain never to captain Australia. His colourful private life was possibly a bar. Instead Ian Johnson was preferred. At a public function where Ian made a typically diplomatic speech, Keith spoke next and said, 'You've just heard our skipper give an excellent speech. It's amazing really because back in Australia he's a cattle farmer. He ships bull to England. In fact he's the biggest bull-shipper in Australia.'

But I digress. In March 1972, thanks to Allen, I saw the Chelsea–Stoke League Cup Final at Wembley. Chelsea were the favourites but Stoke won 2–1 thanks to a late goal by George Eastham. Afterwards we went to my old haunt, The Century, for a drink hoping to catch the train back after the crowd had dispersed. No chance, half of Wembley was in the pub. Allen and I stood in one corner next to a Stoke supporter who was quietly drinking his pint whilst the majority in the pub were Chelsea supporters acting as if they had won. There was no physical intimidation but nevertheless it was scary.

In the summer of 1972 the Australians arrived under a brash new captain, Ian Chappell with a tearaway fast bowler in Denis Lillee. I went to Saturday's play of the Lord's Test with two colleagues from International Life, John Porter and Pat Longhurst. After the match our wives were to join us together with another colleague John Skinner, a bachelor. John hated cricket, being a rugby fan. He chose an Italian restaurant in Twickenham for our post-match meal. Pat had a 1955 Ford Anglia which had broken down and I had lent him my first car a 1954 Ford Anglia, which I had bought for £50 to learn to drive. Pat collected it the night before the match and I suspect we went to Twickenham in it, I cannot remember. The Australian first innings ended early during the day, Greg Chappell scoring an elegant hundred. We were anticipating our first look at Dennis Lillee and he certainly had Geoff Boycott in all sorts of trouble. But the real magic was at the other end. We were sitting at square leg position and in no position to judge the prodigious amount of swing Bob Massie was getting. We guessed from the reactions of the batsmen. John Edrich shouldered arms to a ball well outside the off stump only to see it dart back and take out his middle stump. Mike Smith played Massie best: he took a single off the first ball and then watched it all from the other end. He scored 17 runs that way. Massie took eight wickets in that innings, to add to the eight he took in the first. I doubt if he took another sixteen wickets in his entire Test career.

When we got to the Italian restaurant I was dared to eat a pickled gherkin. I can't stand the things but a dare is a dare. I took the smallest one on offer and tried to swallow it. Alas it was too big for my gullet. There followed an awful couple of minutes when it would go half-way down my gullet and then up and then down again and then up again, all the time to loud sounds of choking and much dribbling. The restaurant management were alarmed, not for my well being but in case their other clients thought it was a reflection on their food. Eventually with one big push the gherkin sped out of my mouth like a projectile and embedded itself in the dessert trolley, in the tiramisu, I think.

In August 1972 Kadeeja and I at last moved into our first house in Stanmore, Middlesex. All our worldly goods did not fill a small van. We had ordered furniture to arrive on the day we moved in. The G-Plan three piece suite we'd ordered turned out to be too big to go through the narrow hall. We had to take it through the shared drive into the back garden, open the back door of the through-lounge and force it in by tilting it. It was deep red in colour and dominated our lounge. Unfortunately the bed didn't arrive so we had to go back to our previous place to spend another night there.

Not only were we the first Asians on the street, we were the only couple under forty-five. Many families had been there since their houses were built in the nineteen-thirties. The house was a half-hour walk from the nearest tube station. I was still learning to drive.

In September, Zamin, our first child, a boy, arrived. The joy of parent-hood has to be experienced, it cannot be described. Every day brought something new to learn; for Kadeeja and I, the parents that is. Not surprisingly my recollections of the next few years are more about my family than about cricket; but they are outside the scope of this book.

What was sad was that the links with my friends from the Northern became weaker. We all got married, (Allen later than others), lived miles away from each other and, no longer working for the same firm, met only occasionally. Eric moved back to Scotland, met and married Morag Fotheringham, another actuarial student. He gave up his studies and moved into the sales side where he cut an unlikely but successful figure. Eric had a butterfly mind and would come up with the most obscure facts with which to regale you. Colin married Sandy and set up home first in Kingston and then in Cobham. Alas, Sandy died in 1986. Kevin married Teresa and settled down in Crawley. Allen stayed single for the longest but then found a girlfriend, Christine. They lived together for a long while before getting married in 1999. Mashuque had returned to Bangladesh (as it was to become shortly) to take part in the freedom movement. He kept in touch for a year or so but then we lost contact. We suspect that he was a casualty in the freedom movement. The one person I did keep in regular touch with was my former flatmate Naseem, who married Jill but stayed in North London, first Goff's Oak and then Enfield.

In 1972 International Life arranged a squash tournament, open to all employees. We had one colleague, Rob Merrick, with thick glasses and spindly legs and heavily strapped knees, who allegedly was of county standard. That's what was said, but this sceptical actuary was not fooled. How could such an unathletic bundle of bones be any good? I didn't have to wait long to find out as I was drawn against him in the first round. A system of handicapping applied, called hands and legs, if I remember correctly. Rob had no handicap, but I had the highest of eight hands and eight legs. Basically I started each set 8–0 up and the other guy had to win eight consecutive points before he scored whereas I scored normally. The only snag was that he was given the first serve in each game. I lost 10–8, 10–8, 10–8. I couldn't win two consecutive points. He just stood in the middle and anticipated every move of mine while I dashed from end to end like a squirrel trapped in a cage. Never in the field of sporting endeavour has someone expended so much energy for so little reward; not even Chuck Fleetwood-Smith who had analysis of 0–298 in the Oval Test of 1938.

In the winter of 1972/3 Pakistan toured Australia and lost 3–0 a series they should have won 2–1 with a little more self-belief. At least Majid broke his duck with a magnificent 158 in Melbourne. There followed a successful tour of New Zealand during which it was announced that Majid would replace Intikhab as skipper for the imminent home series against England. Intikhab was a poor captain, but Majid did not show much initiative either. At least it gave rise to a potential quiz question, 'When did Glamorgan provide the captain for both sides in a Test match?'

9. 1973–1975

Something surprising happened in 1973. Egypt fought Israel; nothing new in that but this time the Israelis came second. It didn't just surprise the Israelis, it surprised the Arabs and, indeed, the whole world. I remember the sort of jokes that were doing the rounds a year earlier. A typical one was that the Egyptian army got an intelligence report that an Israeli soldier was hiding behind the bushes in the desert. So the Egyptian general sent a platoon to flush him out and arrest him. Two days later, just one badly injured soldier returned, the remnant of the platoon.

'What happened? You didn't lose him did you?'

'No, the intelligence was wrong.'

'Why, couldn't you find him?'

'We found him all right, but there were two of them.'

Whilst the world was adjusting to it, OPEC, the consortium of oil-producing countries jacked up the price of oil four-fold. There was inflation in the price of food; Government bonds and share prices plummeted down, down, down. There was a run on Derby Building Society, some commercial banks failed, some major life-insurance companies would have failed if the regulators at the time had been as unbending as their successor Financial Services Authority were when the stock-market crashed a decade ago. Unemployment reached record levels and small business were failing at a record rate.

Many of us genuinely believed that this was the end of the Western world as we knew it. International Life had its own problems and extricated itself from the clasp of IOS and became owned by Keyser Ullman and changed its name to Cannon. Keyser Ullman, a secondary bank was soon to have its own problems.

I had my first taste of managing people when I was put in charge of the Pensions Department, which dealt with all the pension schemes we had set up for clients. Looking back, I was popular but not very effective. I'd never even been a monitor or prefect at school so leadership skills had to be learnt on the hoof. I was in my mid-twenties and had to be agony-aunt to much older people. Believe me there were problems galore. Perhaps the people who lived and worked in suburban Wembley were different to those who worked in the City; perhaps the sixties had a bad image and the seventies were more raunchy; perhaps it was neither, but I had grown up and noticed things more. But there were far more affairs and infidelities amongst my colleagues than there were in the Northern.

In my department there was a lady, in her early forties, very attractive and immaculately dressed who had been through a bruising divorce and was very anti-men. Nevertheless, she advanced a theory that monogamy was wrong but so was promiscuity. What woman needed was serial monogamy. She reckoned that every woman should have six men during her lifetime. One during the late teens for 'exploration', one in the early twenties to have fun and sex, one in her late twenties/thirties to provide the right genes for her children, another for the next twenty years to provide income to look after her and her brood (and plenty of sex). A fifth when her children had flown the nest and finally, in her seventies, a rich older man, or, preferably, a gay toy boy (so that sex was not an issue), rich enough to look after her in her old age. A toy boy was preferable as an older man is unlikely to last long.

Another member of my team was Larry Mitchell who was descended from English parents who settled in India in the nineteenth century. Larry had been a tea salesman in the Nilgiris, in Southern India, but had emigrated to England in 1962. He took a job as an insurance salesman but switched to an admin job in his late fifties. It did not suit him as he was a salesman at heart who loved to talk rather than do paperwork. He used to come to me straight after lunch, a file tucked in his armpit and say, 'Right, I'm off to the Accounts Department to sort out some problems with this client'. One day the HR Manager was coming back after a business lunch and drove into the office car park at around three o'clock. She saw Larry slumped over the steering wheel, his mouth open and his arms splayed. Thinking the he'd had a heart attack on duty, she panicked and called an ambulance. He was rushed to the nearest A&E and he was kept there for a few days.

We gave him early retirement and afterwards he invited Kadeeja and me to his home in New Malden for tea. He then confessed that he used to disappear after lunch for a kip. When the HR manager thought that he had a heart attack, he had no option but to go along with it.

Meanwhile, as learner parents, we were getting great pleasure out of Zamin. He was a very fast learner. He had his own passport by the time he was two. The photograph shows his lips pursed as we'd just taken the dummy out of his mouth but he was able to 'sign', i.e. write his name on the passport. It wasn't very tidy but the letters were clear. By the age of two he knew all the letters of the alphabet. Just before his second birthday I bought him a Fisher Price xylophone where each of the keys had a different colour. I went on a two-day course on Risk Theory at the University of Essex. When I got back he knew all the colours.

He got into the habit of not going to bed before I had read or recited him a story. If it was a story that I made up, I would often vary it and he'd catch me out. I went through a spell when I was busy at work and just wanted to put my feet up. So when he asked for a story, I said, 'tomorrow'. Tomorrow came and he eagerly waited in bed to hear it. Again I said, 'tomorrow'. He didn't complain but when the same thing happened the following evening, he asked me, 'Today's tomorrow or tomorrow's tomorrow.' Bit subtle, I thought.

Mind you, he could occasionally embarrass me. In 1974, we had at last bought new carpets and a new colour television. It was winter morning and I was washing my pride and joy, the Renault 12. Zamin was with me using the chamois leather to dry the car when a neighbour walked past with a daughter of a similar age to Zamin. Whilst I exchanged pleasantries with the neighbour, the two kids eyed each other. Zamin was the first to speak and it was a long speech with pauses:

'I'm Zamin. This is MY Dad. This is our car. We've got new carpets and curtains. We've got a new TV. It shows pictures in colour.'

With tensions at work and excitement at home, it is not surprising that I have little personal recollection of the 1973 Test series. Rohan Kanhai, a brilliant, aggressive, risk-taking batsman turned out to be a risk-averse and ruthless captain. Gradually Ray Illingworth's team of elderly cricketers was dismantled. In the final Test, at nearly close of play, Geoff Boycott got out to an atypically intemperate shot. Illingworth suspected that Boycott was eying his job. In a typically British compromise, the selectors chose Mike Denness as the captain for the winter tour of the West Indies, a left-field appointment for sure. That tour was the making of Dennis Amiss and Tony Greig. Boycott had a dreadful time until the final Test. My hero Garry Sobers went out with a whimper.

My interest in cricket was revived next year when Pakistan toured England again. They were one fast bowler short of being a great team; one fast bowler, self-belief and a good captain that is. Still, they went through the tour undefeated. Zaheer Abbas scored another double hundred but I've never warmed to him, stylish like a right-handed Gower but supremely selfish.

For me, the two standout memories were of Majid Khan. His 98 in the Oval Test, treating Willis with contempt, and then missing a sweep off a straight ball from Derek Underwood when on 98; and his 109 in the first one-day international; an unbelievable knock. I've got the century on DVD and live in hope that one day ESPN will broadcast the 98. It was interesting to watch the century again, as I did last week, and contrast the reality with the vision stored in your memory. Majid was certainly very elegant and a timer and caresser rather than hitter, but he had a lower back-lift than Sobers, Gower, Zaheer and Lara.

Before the Oval Test I watched a very painful Wimbledon. My boyhood tennis hero, Ken Rosewall, never won Wimbledon before he turned pro in his early twenties and then missed the best twelve years because Wimbledon was amateur only. Since 1968 he had contested but never got to the final. He had the best service return in the business but he had to as his service was weak. This year he got to the final and the entire universe bar one person was rooting for him. That one person was Jimmy Connors whom he had to face in the final. Jimmy murdered him. It was sad.

The 1974 football World Cup was another disappointment. England failed to qualify so I switched my support to Scotland. They failed to progress beyond Round 1 so I switched to Holland who were playing the best football but they lost to Germany in the final. So I gave up football and returned to cricket.

I followed the Lillee and Thomson series which evoked memories of Frank Tyson in 1954/5. But there was a difference. This was raw aggression. Thomson said he liked the sight of the batsman's blood. He certainly had the batsmen cowering. Fred Titmus, sans four toes, was asked to open the innings and before then Cowdrey was flown out from Surrey to get into line. He was game but he merely delayed the inevitable.

1975 was the year when the first cricket World Cup was staged in England. John Woodcock made Australia and Pakistan the two favourites. Kadeeja was at an advanced stage of pregnancy, so I followed the games on television/radio and *The Times*. The teams were divided into two groups. One group comprised, Australia, West Indies, Pakistan and Sri Lanka; the other England, New Zealand, India and East Africa.

Asif Iqbal was the new captain of Pakistan and Intikhab Alam was omitted. Its batting, Majid Khan, Sadiq Mohammed, Zaheer Abbas, Mushtaq Mohammed, Asif Iqbal, Wasim Raja, a seventeen-year-old Javed Miandad and Imran Khan was one of the strongest in the tournament but its bowling was weak. In its first game Australia rattled up 278. In reply, Majid played a glittering innings of 65 full of delicious late cuts and hooks but wickets kept falling at the other end. Then straight after tea, in sweeping Ashley Mallett, Majid feathered a catch to Rodney Marsh and walked. That then brought Asif, ever a man for a crisis, together with Wasim Raja. For a change Wasim batted responsibly in a support role. Together they put on a half-century stand and we dared to think of victory. However, the early batsmen had left too much to do, the asking rate was too much. Dennis Lillee returned and that was that.

My daughter Deena was born. Northwick Park discharged Kadeeja from the maternity ward after thirty-six hours. So, with my son Zamin excited at the prospect of having a sister, I brought mother and daughter home. It was the day Pakistan was playing West Indies. If they lost they were out of the World Cup. I had the television on all the time whilst I tried to juggle my duties as husband and father with the temptations of a fan. As Kadeeja has frequently reminded me since then, the fan on the whole won. Asif Iqbal had been hospitalised (appendicitis) and Majid Khan took over as captain. Pakistan batted first and Majid Khan, Mushtaq Mohammed and Wasim Raja all contributed fifties as the team rattled up 266. When West Indies batted Sarfraz Nawaz in one of the greatest spells of World Cup bowling made deep incisions into the strong batting line up. One by one, Gordon Greenidge, Roy Fredericks and Alvin Kallicharan fell trying to make haste. Rohan Kanhai and Clive Lloyd had a stand playing with a little more care but then both were out;

ninety-nine for five. Then Viv Richards and Bernard Julien fell; 151 for 7. Eventually, at quarter to seven they were nine down, Derek Murray and Andy Roberts batting, with sixty-four to get and the match was as good as in the Pakistani bag. At that point the coverage ceased on both television and radio. I returned to family duties content that the match was won. Even Pakistan couldn't contrive to lose the match.

Imagine my consternation when I read in *The Times* the next morning that West Indies had won and Pakistan were out of the World Cup. It was scarcely credible. Majid had correctly decided to bowl West Indies out. He used up his four main bowlers and had to make up the fifth bowler from a combination of Miandad, Wasim Raja, leg spinners both. When the match got to the sixtieth over, he had to call upon Wasim Raja. Looking back, Murray and Roberts were the coolest characters in the West Indian line up. The result was the biggest shock of my career as a fan. You don't support Pakistan without suffering pain along the way. World Cup semi-final 1979, Sydney 1973, Hobart 1999, World Cup Final 1999 but none could compare with this game against West Indies. Only two other events, England's capitulation at Adelaide in 2006/7 and the *News of the World* sting on Mohammad Amir *et al.* in 2010 have since equalled it in shock value. It was no consolation to read John Woodcock's article in *The Times* say that he was disappointed that the team that had given him the greatest pleasure was now out of the tournament.

England had a comparatively smooth ride to the semi-finals. They scored a mountain of runs and then, facing 300-odd to get, India replied with 136–3. Gavaskar batted through 60 overs to score 36. I'm a great admirer of his, even though I dislike other similar batsmen such as Hanif and Boycott. He was however prone to being slighted all too readily.

In the semi-finals, England were blown away by Gary Gilmour (6–14). All out for nintey-three, Snow and Old struck back and it looked if England might still make it to the final. Wrong. Gilmour came to the party, this time as a batsman, scoring an unbeaten twenty-eight.

So it was an Australia *v.* West Indies final and a thrilling match it was too. West Indies batted first and Lillee bowled at great pace. Fredericks hooked him for six but he slipped and dislodged the bails. Greenidge and Kallicharan did not last long, so that when Lloyd joined Kanhai, the game was in the balance. They put on 149, Lloyd's savagery being complemented by Kanhai's watchfulness. Australia had to get 292 to win. Wickets fell at regular intervals, no-one making a big score, Greg Chappell's sixty-two being the highest. There were four run-outs, many by Viv Richards. They were sixty runs adrift when Lillee, the last man, joined Thomson. They got to within eighteen of the target.

After that there was a four-Test series. In the first, Lillee and Thomson reprised their heroics of the previous Ashes series and effectively ended Denness's career, Tony Greig taking over. The summer was however dominated by an unlikely star, a grey-haired bank clerk, or that's what he looked like: David Steele. He had a grand summer.

Zamin had been very excited at the arrival of a sister. She came with a balloon and a small plastic bike. He didn't ask how mummy carried all that in her tummy. He proudly displayed his sister to visitors. That lasted a couple of days until he realised that mum was going to spend more time with her. He wasn't happy about that and for a while he was closer to me, but not for long. The bond of a child with his mother is very strong.

With two children I became more like a family man. We had several friends with young kids of similar ages. Kadeeja was constantly teaching me to say the right things to our Asian friends. The problem was that I didn't fit the standard template. No other Asian would have written this book; or put it another way, they'd have written a different book. Anyone who reads this book would conclude that I was a hapless buffoon. A typical Asian would never subscribe to that. He's successful and so are his spouse and kids. Nothing goes wrong with their holidays, they stay in the best hotels and eat in the best restaurants.

There's a story of an Asian lady who was distraught when she realised that hers was the only house on the street that hadn't been burgled. 'People will think I have nothing worth stealing.' She put it about that she too had been burgled and that her loss was greater as she hadn't been insured.

Kadeeja often pleaded with me, 'OK, you don't have to show off but at least keep quiet about your gaffes.'

10. 1976–1978

On Boxing Day (1975) Lance Gibbs had taken his 308th Test wicket, one more than Fred. TMS woke up Fred and asked for his views. He grumbled and said something like, 'He'd never have caught up with me. I should've had 450 if it wasn't for the gin brigade at the MCC. I missed thirty Test matches and two tours.' Not a word of praise for Lance.

I sometimes think Yorkshire cricketers are born miserable. When Colin Cowdrey died, *Wisden Cricket Monthly* sought the views of several cricketers on Colin the player and Colin the man. The standard approach on such occasions is to dwell on their achievements and downplay their foibles. All Ray Illingworth seemed to be saying was, 'I was a better captain than him.'

Next summer, 1976, was the start of the period of West Indian domination. Clive Lloyd, smarting from the defeat inflicted by the pace and intimidation of Denis Lillee and Jeff Thomson decided that the way to take on the world was to take the Aussie model to its limit. He was able to do that because he had a battery of fast bowlers, starting with two of the highest quality in Andy Roberts and Mike Holding supported by Wayne Daniel and Vanburn Holder. He made fitness and discipline key requirements and got rid of Keith Boyce who had created problems the previous winter. Over the next few years more fast bowlers would emerge, one of the highest class (Joel Garner) and others who were very good, Colin Croft and Sylvester Clarke. He also had Viv Richards, battle-hardened and in the middle of his best run of form.

The atmosphere was hostile. A white South African blonde with an incomplete command of English was trying to say that West Indian teams wilt under pressure. Instead he said that they had a tendency to grovel. Frank Worrell or Garry Sobers would have ignored that remark. Not Clive Lloyd and certainly not Viv Richards. They went out of their way to intimidate batsmen physically. The sight of Tony Greig, six feet seven, made them crank up their speed and bowl fast yorkers. More than once he couldn't get his bat down in time. Mike Holding and Andy Roberts's assault on John Edrich and Brian Close went beyond the limits of physical intimidation into unfair play. The umpires ought to have intervened.

At the Oval we saw two performances that must rank in the top two dozen ever and a third that was exceptional. The first two were Richards's 291 and Holdings's fourteen wickets on a flat pitch. The third was Denis Amiss's 205.

I must admit that I didn't enjoy the West Indian style of play. They slowed the over rate down and made bowling monotonous. But what I disliked most was that their approach was racist. They regarded cricket as a vehicle for vanquishing the white man. In fact Richards talked of African domination, disenfranchising the large Asian and white communities in the West Indies (Rohan Kanhai, Alvin Kallicharan, Sonny Ramadhin, Jeff Stollmeyer, Gerry Gomez, Jackie Hendricks). Racism does not become legitimate just because it is black people who're practising it.

That winter we combined two years' annual leave to visit Pakistan and India in December/ January to visit both sets of in-laws who were eagerly awaiting a sight of their first grandchildren. Before we went, New Zealand toured Pakistan and we saw the rise of a future star, Javed Miandad. Pakistan had a new captain, Mushtaq Mohammed. In the Karachi Test Majid Khan joined an elite group of three Australians, Victor Trumper, Charlie Macartney and Don Bradman, who've scored a century before lunch on the opening day of a Test match.

The series was played against a backdrop of dispute on pay between the players and the Pakistan Cricket Board's chief, Hafeez Kardar. Kardar reacted by sacking the team selected to tour Australia and naming a new team led by Intikhab Alam. In the event, greater powers prevailed and Kardar had to back down. The episode did a lot to bind the team together and enhanced the authority of Mushtaq Mohammed, who turned out to be the most effective captain since, well Kardar actually.

The first Test was drawn but the second was lost heavily following a second innings collapse. When the Third started we were on our way from India to Pakistan and I missed most of it. This was the Test when Imran became a genuine fast bowler and took twelve wickets. After a good opening knock by Majid, Asif supported by Haroon Rashid gained a healthy lead and when Australia collapsed again Pakistan needed just thirty-two to win. By then I was with my parents and able to watch the end on Pakistan TV. Lillee bowled furiously and fast and cowed Sadiq and Zaheer. I was terrified that we'd capitulate again and fail to achieve the nominal target. But Majid stood firm and hit an unbelievable six off Lillee and saw Pakistan through. There was much rejoicing on Pakistan TV. The broadcaster was an old class-mate of mine in Karachi Grammar School, Chishty Mujahid. We were together in the sixth form, though he was an arts student and I a maths/science student. That win was a seminal one and was the springboard for the rise of Imran and a new era for Pakistan.

It was good to see both sets of parents. Mine were living in Rawalpindi so I could revisit old haunts. The first thing that struck me was that distances were much shorter than I remembered; no doubt because I was travelling by car rather than on 9–13-year-old feet. Another was that throughout Pakistan there had been a process of de-Anglicisation so that we no longer saw Gough Road or McLeod Road or Frere Street or Napier Barracks. They were replaced by Muslim names. The country was striving to find its own identity. Shalwar-kameez was taking over from shirt-trousers. The first steps were being taken towards giving Islam greater prominence. At the political level, this was no doubt motivated by the new found oil wealth of the Middle East. Family friends were asking me, 'Do you fast? Do you say your prayers?' instead of asking, 'Do you lead a good life? Are you honest in all your dealings?' Form seemed more important than content.

Pakistan went on to tour to the West Indies and lost a closely fought series 2–1. The batting was carried by Majid and Wasim Raja. Pakistan should have won the first Test but, as in the World Cup match in 1975, they could not split the last pair. The second Test was lost, new fast bowler Colin Croft claiming eight for thirty-three. The third Test was drawn, Majid scoring a magnificent 167. Mushtaq, of late so nervous against fast bowling, at last came into his own with bat and ball in the fourth Test. With Majid scoring ninety-two, the fourth Test was won so the two teams were one all as they went to Kingston.

Throughout this series the batting had relied upon Majid and his strength against fast bowling. Before the fifth Test, a newspaper article quoted Mushtaq as saying that Andy Roberts threw his faster ball.

Although Mushtaq denied having said it, it fired up Roberts. After Imran had got West Indies out for a low score (might have been lower still but for Greenidge's 102), Roberts bowled at the speed of light to Majid who did not see the ball on a couple of occasions. Not surprisingly this shook him and he was soon out and fear spread through the entire batting line up. Asif scored a century in the second innings, his only decent innings in the series, but the match was lost.

We now reach the period, 1977, when, with the arrival of Kerry Packer, cricket lost its innocence. The establishment took an immediate dislike to him. My attitude was one of ambivalence. On the one hand, I believed that cricketers were underpaid and fully supported anything that improved their lot. On the other, I wanted to avoid any schism which would damage the great game and my enjoyment of it; the same selfish approach that led me to oppose Peter Hain. I was anti-Tony Greig and Asif Iqbal for going behind the back of their employers. Mind you, there were many people taking selfish positions. I remember Graham Roope strongly supporting the exclusion of those who'd sided with Packer and thinking, 'You would, wouldn't you.' Later on, Marsh and Lillee made Kim Hughes's life a misery because he hadn't sided with Packer.

England were lucky in that it had two outstanding youngsters, Ian Botham and David Gower, whom they could fast track as a result; a cerebral captain in Mike Brearley to take over and a couple of other authentic Test players in Graham Gooch and Bob Willis. Australia suffered the most, but Pakistan lost Asif Iqbal, Majid Khan, Imran Khan, Zaheer Abbas and Mushtaq Mohammed, their five key players.

It was against this background that Greg Chappell brought a team to England. Tony Greig had been replaced as captain by Mike Brearley but kept his place in the team. It was a low-key series which England won. There were two memorable achievements, both in the Nottingham Test. The first was the return to Test cricket of Boycott which he crowned by scoring his hundredth first class hundred – but he only got there by running out Randall in his own selfish way. The other event was Botham making his Test debut and taking five wickets in Australia's first innings. He started as he meant to go on by dismissing Greg Chappell with an innocuous delivery.

Next year Pakistan and New Zealand toured. Pakistan, without any Packer players, got slaughtered by England, Botham giving astonishing exhibitions of swing bowling and Gower lighting up our lives with his sublime timing.

These two transformed the texture of the English cricket team. No longer would it be the Malvolian self-denial of Boycott or the introspection characterised by Colin Cowdrey of days just gone. Brearley was introducing a more cerebral approach to captaincy, but it was Gower and Botham who were the defining individuals of the change in the team's cricket.

There has been no English cricketer like Botham and that was why even in his pomp, when he routinely walked on water, he was admired not loved. He was brash, he was utterly self-confident, he was Australian by temperament. We have no reliable way of comparing him with W. G. Grace, whose best days were behind him before Test cricket began, but Botham was certainly the greatest and most influential English cricketer since him and, indeed, the most feared cricketer anywhere since Bradman. Was he the best all-rounder ever? Well, as I shall argue later, he wasn't even the best of his era but that is largely due to reckless dissipation of his prodigious natural talent. I would say that he was the most influential English cricketer ever. If you compiled a list of such individuals they would, in my opinion, comprise: W. G. Grace, Wilfred Rhodes, Jack Hobbs, Wally Hammond, Denis Compton, Len Hutton, Alec Bedser, Peter May and Fred Trueman. Botham would lead that company.

However, the person I warmed to was not him but David Gower. Just as Majid was about to go into decline a successor came along. Gower was a left-handed Majid, a languid timer and caresser of the ball. It was typical of him that he began his Test career by pulling the first ball he faced for four. Equally typical were the three or four low scores that followed.

There was a frailty about his batting which made you savour it, even more for the fear that it could not last. He would regale us with half an hour of sublime artistry only then to get out to a wild swing. However, it would be wrong to suggest that all he was capable of were cameos. His overall Test average was better than that of Gooch. More importantly he's played several critical and long innings: 1. At Kingston in 1981, he batted nearly eight hours to score an unbeaten 154 against the fearsome West Indian pace quartet; and 2. In the 1984 tour of Pakistan he scored 152 at Faisalabad and 173 not out at Lahore, successfully saving both Tests.

Gower was also the best fielder in the cover region that I've seen, better than Colin Bland. Bob Simpson once explained that a good cover fielder needs an instinctive sense of geometry to determine the best point at which to intercept the ball. You are travelling in one straight line and the ball in another; both are travelling at different speeds. You have to determine the line you must traverse so as to arrive at the intersection at the same time as the ball. Gower had that skill and would always get to the ball without appearing to stretch himself, unlike someone such as Derek Randall, another brilliant fielder, who runs at breakneck speed after the ball to retrieve it near or beyond the boundary ropes. There you can see the effort. With Gower you don't. The art that conceals art, as Neville Cardus used to say, although in this case it is art that conceals science. The same was true of his batting and he was unfairly blamed for lack of effort. Give me a Gower instead of a Gooch any day.

Pakistan were able to include all its Packer players when India toured Pakistan in 1978/79 to play a three-Test series. India was captained by Bishen Bedi and Pakistan by Mushtaq Mohammed, two team-mates from Northamptonshire. The fabled spin quartet was ageing and Kapil Dev was just beginning. So Pakistan toppled several batting records and won the series 2–0.

In 1978/79 Mike led England to a 5–1 win against an Australian side shorn of Packer players. Gower and Randall were the main run-getters, each scoring a century. Brearley himself and Geoff Boycott had poor tours and Botham, by his standards, an average one although he was the leading wicket-taker. For Australia a new bowling star appeared in the form of Rodney Hogg who took forty wickets.

Australia played a two Test series against Pakistan immediately afterwards. In the first Majid scored a sublime century but the Aussies were well placed on the final day with only seventy-seven to get, with seven wickets left. Sarfraz then had an amazing spell of what we now call reverse swing of five wickets for one run and Australia lost by seventy-one runs. In all, he took nine wickets in the innings. Australia won the second Test and Majid got a pair.

The 1970s were drawing to a close. For me, it was an extended transition from the carefree youth of the sixties to adult responsibilities of the eighties. Of the five decades of my adulthood, from the 60s to the 00s, if the 60s was the most fun-filled, the 70s was the most soulless. That is the verdict of hindsight. Back then, in 1978, my priority was to get another job as Cannon was going nowhere.

11. 1979–1983

In December 1978 I joined Sun Life. It was a major change as I was to be part of the marketing rather than the actuarial team. The people who interviewed me were Peter Pummell, who was to become my boss, and Norman King who was on the Board of Sun Life. The offer letter came from Norman King and I phoned him to say that the terms were acceptable, could he send me a formal contract to sign.

'Contract, what do you want a contract for?'

'Well, your letter just talks of salary and there's a lot of detail which would be covered in a formal contract.'

'Such as?'

'Such as holidays, pension rights, notice period and many more.'

'Oh they're all in the 'I for P', you can read them when you join us.'

'Don't you think I should see them first?'

'I don't see why, they're pretty standard.'

'I'd still like to know. What's 'I for P', by the way?'

'Instructions for Procedure.'

That was as clear as mud. Anyway, I had a chat with Peter and decided to accept it. Norman King had a formal air but was a lovely individual, an old-fashioned Englishman who never swore. He loved tennis and amateur opera and participated in both. Once he was playing doubles and ran back to the baseline to reach an overhead lob. When he realised that he couldn't make it he wanted to tell his partner and shouted at the top of his voice, 'Can't'. That was misheard and the players had to stop as they couldn't control their laughter. One day he was returning from Bristol in heavy rain for choir practice in Guildford when, on the M4, a lorry going the other way came across the central reservation and pulped his car. Norman could only be identified from his dental records.

Norman's successor was Frank Berry whose qualities I admired but came to appreciate even more after I had left Sun Life. He was a conciliator,

107

whereas most people from a sales background are confrontational.

Sun Life dealt exclusively through brokers and transacted traditional types of life insurance and pensions business. They wished to move into the new types of products that Cannon used to sell. The work was interesting but there was little difference to my social life.

1979 was the year of the second World Cup which had some memorable matches. I missed most of the tournament because I was in India attending my second and third sisters' weddings.

Something important happened on 14th May 1979, right in the middle of the World Cup. Maggie Thatcher came into power. After some teething problems, she imposed changes that reshaped the economy and the public's attitude to wealth creation. The pain came first and there was deep recession. The miners' strike followed and her stock was low.

Had she not won the Falklands war enabling her to be re-elected on the back of euphoria and jingoism, she could quite probably not have won a second term. So chance saved her from being consigned to a footnote in history. Instead she became a major agent for change. Churchill once said, 'I'll have a very important role in the History of Britain as I intend to write it.' Maggie could have said, 'I intend to make history.'

During July David Gower put on a six-hour display of exhilarating batsmanship, scoring exactly 200. More circumspect than normal, his exceptional timing was there for all to see, during the First Test against India. Then, when the summer had nearly gone, I saw one of the greatest innings it's been my privilege to watch: Sunil Gavasker's 221 at the Oval. He'd been petulant all summer. However, Brearley had presented him with a challenge. Set to get 438 in the fourth innings, effectively the tallest winning score ever if they got there, he batted with such skill and control that the opening pair added 213 before Chetan Chauhan fell for eighty. Dilip Vangsarkar joined Gavaskar and the scoring rate was increased. At tea they had crossed 300 and the further 130-odd that was required seemed eminently feasible. England cynically slowed the over rate down, so that in the last twenty overs 110 were needed. At one stage Botham dropped Vengsarkar, which seemed a good omen, for the Indians. The score had reached 366 before Vengsarkar was out. The captain probably erred in sending Kapil Dev ahead of Vishwanath. Still, Gavaskar carried on. However, at 389, shortly after a drinks break, Gavaskar was out. Botham took two key wickets and despite valiant efforts India finished eight short.

That winter Mike Brearley took a team to play a full strength Australia and lost the three Test series 3–0. He was worried about his poor batting form being targeted by the barrackers. As a camouflage he grew a thick beard. So they called him the Ayatullah, Ayatullah Khomeini being in the news, having assumed power in Iran.

During the same winter, Pakistan toured India and lost the series. More important, the great team of the seventies was breaking up. Mushtaq had already been dropped. Majid had a poor series but not as poor as Zaheer Abbas who was convinced that someone had put a spell on him. The batting was carried by Javed Miandad and Wasim Raja. Kapil Dev outshone a half-fit Imran. Gavaskar ground out centuries.

In 1980 Sun Life relocated me to Bristol and in September I moved to lovely Sneyd Park. We had a great house and fantastic neighbours. It remains the place Kadeeja loved most. I formed a fresh circle of friends.

One of these was Brim Avery. He and I went, with a journalist, to the second day of the Lord's Test against the West Indies. On the first day Gooch had scored a brilliant century. On the second day Richards scored a bigger and more brilliant century. I thought there was a touch of the sadist in him. I don't know what Bob Willis had said to him but he took his bowling apart. England had two brilliant outfielders: Gower and Randall, but neither was playing. Richards singled out the flat-footed Woolmer and Underwood and placed the ball just out of their reach but with sufficient momentum to make them run all the way to the fence thinking that they could get there.

1981 had the riveting Wimbledon final between Bjorn Borg and John McEnroe, the monarch versus the usurper, Mr Ice Cool versus the Brat. Borg had won the previous five Wimbledons and was not going to surrender the title in a hurry. McEnroe, apart from playing scintillating tennis, tried all sorts of subterfuges and delaying tactics to unsettle Borg. But Borg would not be distracted. His concentration was intense and came through the television tube. In the end McEnroe just sneaked through to a win. It was the end of an era.

But tennis was a side show that year. 1981 was the year Charles married Diana. Who can forget the vision of a radiant Princess on the Palace balcony? The wedding day was a public holiday and BBC had a record number of viewers. Not everyone watched, though. The wedding day coincided with the Southport festival and Southport had its best gate ever as all the Lancastrian blokes left their wives to watch the wedding and went to watch the cricket.

But even the royal wedding was a side-show that year. 1981 was Botham's year. There is no point in reliving an oft-told tale, most recently related in a new book, *500 to 1*. His achievements were so staggering that you couldn't put them in a novel, as people would say they were non-credible. Graham Gooch once asked him who wrote his scripts.

One fact that is often overlooked is how poor a series Gower and Gooch, not to mention Gatting, had. We were holidaying in Cornwall when the famous Headingley Test was played. I only read afterwards that Ladbrokes were offering 500 to 1 against an England win. I'm not a betting man and I doubt that I'd have placed a bet had I known the odds, but it bugs me that I didn't have the option.

That series did untold harm to English cricket. Botham came to believe that he could walk on water. By all accounts he was a law unto himself and was difficult to manage. He lived life to the full. David Gower described him as an all-rounder in the widest sense of the term. Botham had his own cronies and he could be very generous with them. A big man, he could be physically intimidating to those outside his charmed circle. It is interesting to watch Nasser Hussain and Ian Botham commentate together on Sky. Nasser is obviously not a groupie and there is definite needle between them, stemming I think from Nasser's autobiography which was issued just before he joined the Sky team. In it he dismissed Ian's comments as being a waste of time. Why? Because he is always lambasting selectors for not picking someone they hadn't picked without saying whom he would drop to make way.

I can't remember which year exactly, but around 1981 or 1982, my doorbell rang and I found someone collecting in support of Ayatullah Khomeini. I wasn't a supporter of what was going on in Iran but, for a quiet life, I took a fiver out of my wallet and offered it to him. He threw it back at me, 'Shame on you. Is that all you can give?'

I said, 'It's my money and if you don't want it I'll keep it.' I shut the door.

In 1982 I planned to write the History of Pakistan Cricket. In the time-honoured way, I sent the sample early chapters to a number of publishers without luck. I then wrote to David Frith who put me in touch with John Newth of George Allen & Unwin. He was very keen and made several enquiries, but eventually concluded that he was unlikely to sell enough. My problem was that I was a year too late. The book had to be on the market before the 1982 tour.

Bob Willis was appointed captain in 1982, Brearley having retired, again. A bright individual with a good tactical brain, he found it difficult to combine captaincy with fast bowling. He was so 'in the zone' when bowling that he could not think of anything else. When he was resting after bowling it was worse. So, on the field, you got the impression that Gower and Botham were the pilots. He defeated Pakistan in a tightly fought series – more on that later – and took the team to Australia in 1982/3 where they won a thrilling Test but lost two.

The 1980s saw the rise of Imran Khan and with him Pakistan. It was the age of the all-rounders: Botham, Kapil Dev, Imran and Hadlee. Of these, Botham was the most prodigiously gifted with Kapil Dev not far behind. I think success came too soon to Botham and came in such profusion that he thought success was his right. He made his Test debut in 1977 and his peak years were 1978 to 1981, between the ages of 22 to 26, then he declined, at first gradually and then with greater speed. His last Test was in 1992 but, as a bowler, he was a caricature of his true self after 1985. Batsmen played his reputation rather than his residual self. Kapil Dev had to work harder, given the flat pitches and poor fielding that he had to contend with. He, too, reached the top in his early twenties, but he maintained his standards for a very long time. However, the two who through hard work maximised their talents, were Hadlee and Imran. Both were in their late twenties before they hit world-class form, but they kept improving after that. Hadlee was the more skilful bowler but Imran was the better batsman. And, of course, he was an outstanding captain. For that reason, I regard Imran as the best of the 1980s all-rounders, fit to rank second to Sobers. Was he better than Kallis? Kallis is a far superior fielder and on batting/ bowling, whether you use difference in averages (batting average minus bowling average) or ratio (batting average divided by bowling average) Kallis shades him. However, in terms of altering the course of matches, for which there is no measurable statistic, Imran scores higher.

I went to the first day of the Edgbaston Test against Pakistan in 1982. My nine-year-old son Zamin, not a cricket fan but aware of Botham, said to me as I set off, 'My Botham will sort your Imran out.' I was pleased to hear the sentiments as he's a British kid. Not having seen

Pakistan in action live on a British ground since 1967, I was in for a shock. Gone were the days when Pakistan supporters sat quietly in almost English-like silence. No doubt they were inspired by the West Indian crowd. However, where the West Indians were generally good humoured, many of the Pakistani supporters were more aggressive in their taunts. I did not like it. I kept my head down while I watched. England batted first and thanks to a fluent seventy-four from Gower, they seemed to have the upper hand. Imran scored a moral victory against Botham in their personal duel. He ostentatiously placed two deep mid-wickets. You could see from Botham's demeanour that he wanted to plant the ball out of the ground. Imran then bowled a perfect yorker and Botham was far too late on it. He was out for one; which was one more than he would get in the second innings. Reverse swing was an unknown term in those days but Imran came back and cleaned up the innings. He had started the day by clean bowling the makeshift opener Randall as he shouldered arms to a booming in-swinger. Imran finished with seven for fifty-two. There was time for Botham to bowl one over and Mudassar ducked to a good-length ball, believing it to be a beamer and was bowled.

The boorishness of the young Pakistan supporters was threatening to alienate me; as was the gamesmanship of the vice-captain Javed Miandad. In the final Test, David Constant gave Sikandar Bakht, a tail-ender, out caught in the leg trap when he'd clearly missed the ball. Imran made a big issue out of this, blaming Constant for the defeat. Whilst it is true that, had they added another twenty or thirty runs, the outcome would almost certainly have been different, it is the batting that let the team down; and Imran himself leaked runs on the last day in his search for speed on uncertain footholds. Perhaps in his first term as captain, given Pakistan's penchant for regicide, he was keen to shift blame elsewhere. Imran's development from someone who could neither bat nor bowl to the world's leading all-rounder had been achieved through self-analysis and continual self-improvement, so he must have known the real reason for the defeat. But such statements were not helpful with the team and the fans. It gave them an external bogey.

That winter saw Imran at the peak of his bowling powers. He took fifty-three wickets in nine Tests against Australia and India. He actually played second fiddle to Qadir against Australia but when the Indians arrived for a six Test series, he took thirty-three wickets in the first four

Tests in a devastating exhibition of controlled reverse swing. He then went off the boil with what was ultimately diagnosed as a stress fracture of the shin.

Both Australia and India complained about some of the umpiring decisions. Imran, concerned that gloss was being taken off the team's performance, suggested that neutral umpires be used in the future but support was lukewarm, on grounds of cost.

The person who handled Imran best was Mohinder Amarnath. He followed it up with an equally successful series against West Indies in West Indies.

	Tests	Inn	N.O.	Aggregate	H.S.	100s	Average
v. Pakistan	6	10	2	584	120	3	73.00
v. West Indies	5	9	0	598	117	2	66.44
	11	19	2	1182	120	5	69.30

It's a stupendous record against the premier fast bowlers of the time. Both Imran and Clive Lloyd said he was the best player of fast bowling they had seen. He then went to England for the World Cup and was the Man of the Match in the Final. He was on top of the world. But cricket is a funny game. West Indies toured India immediately afterwards and, boy, did they make India pay for daring to beat them in the World Cup Final. Amarnath was humiliated, his record in that series being

Tests	Inn	N.O.	Aggregate	H.S.	100s	Average
3	6	0	1	1	0	0.17

One run in six completed innings, two pairs and a 0 and 1. Compton in 1950/51 (fifty-three in seven completed innings, HS twenty-three not out, average 7.57.and Hammond in 1934 (162 in eight completed innings, HS forty-three and average 20.25) by comparison were quite successful.

One interesting domestic episode helped to keep my feet on the ground. I had received a promotion and a good salary rise. Kadeeja was delighted and Zamin joined in. Deena, being nearly three years younger, didn't say anything. She caught me alone and asked quietly, 'Daddy, have you

been promoted or pensioned?'

Taken aback by this question, I looked to see if she was winding me up. The little angel looked sincere enough, so I told her, 'Promoted, darling.'

She reflected on that and then asked, 'What's the difference?'

What profound thoughts come from the mouth of kids?

On another occasion she was having trouble going to sleep and I was at my limit of telling stories, so I said to her. 'Imagine you're the farmer and you've got sheep in a pen. Count all of them and you'll fall asleep.'

'How do I know that I haven't counted one already?'

'Make them jump over the fence and count them as they do.'

Five minutes later she shouts out from the bedroom, 'Dad, one of them refuses to jump. What shall I do?'

A highlight of the year was a visit by my parents. My father had become disillusioned with Pakistan. The country that he opted for in the expectation of democracy and freedom turned out to be the very opposite. His children were all settled abroad and he wished to return to his native Kerala. He could not, as a Pakistani citizen, do that; the Indian authorities would not permit it. His cunning plan was to emigrate to Canada, where my brother lived, acquire Canadian citizenship and then emigrate to India. He and mum were on their way to Toronto when they stopped over. It was great to see them and great for the children too. Both had visibly aged, particularly Mum, who'd shed her normal plumpness.

Alas, the grand plan was never realised. Within eighteen months both were dead. Mum's loss of weight was caused by stomach cancer which was terminal. Dad couldn't contemplate life without her and actually went first. It took me years to get over the twin loss. Death is so final and irrevocable. You are left with a catalogue of regrets. Things you have said that you shouldn't have. Things you should have but didn't.

12. 1984–1987

At Sun Life there were several young actuaries of a similar age to me. We were friends but also competitors for potential senior positions. However, it was apparent to all that the standout candidate was Les Owen, a scouser without a scouse accent. He had everything: brains, personality and above all, utter self-confidence. He had the Brian Close/Ian Botham quality of unshakeable self-belief. Not surprisingly, he rose to be Chief Executive. I once described him as the Ian Botham of Sun Life and he stopped dead in his tracks and stared at me. I knew exactly what he was thinking, 'What is Icki saying? I'm gifted or I'm a boor?' I met Les again a couple of years ago at a reunion and I said to him, 'Hey, Les, if I told you that the person your first-ever girlfriend had a crush on died recently, what would you say?' He said, 'How would you know who my first girlfriend was. I was in Liverpool and you presumably were in Pakistan?' 'I was in England, actually, but isn't it true that she had a crush on Alan Ball?' Les gave me puzzled look and then in a little while the penny dropped. 'Oh her. Yes. Bloody hell, how did you know that?' He kept harking back to that throughout the day, 'How did Icki know that?' My brain is a repository of useless facts. Les must have mentioned it sometime and I just filed it away, in fact filed it unknowingly.

My problems with public speaking were overcome during the eighties. Sun Life had several accomplished speakers as role models. The best of these was John Woolnough, a good friend and, a perfect human being, who'd get a message across without seeming to do so. (He'd say, with characteristic modesty, that only his Heavenly Father was perfect.) Once we toured the length and breadth of the country giving the same talk to

115

a dozen different audiences, John doing his bit and I mine. I got bored of giving the same talk and varied it, changed jokes, etc. John, having crafted his talk with care, never varied it and made the same joke sound fresh every time. Nothing original in that, stage actors do that all the time. It was a good lesson for me.

On another occasion, I went with him to Leeds to speak at a seminar launching another new product. We arrived the previous evening and had dinner with the Leeds Branch manager in our hotel. John was too busy talking when the waitress came to take the order so he skim-read the menu and opted for roast beef. I, having studied the menu, went for moules marnière. When the dinner arrived, John looked at what I'd selected and started salivating. So I let him have my dinner as I quite liked roast beef anyway. John had a pleasant dinner. That night he was ill. The mussels were 'off'. Good pro that he was, he gave his talk as if nothing had happened, but of course he couldn't see the deathly pallor on his face.

There was another occasion when I went to Aberdeen to give a talk to brokers. I took with me a young colleague from our marketing department; a very capable girl whom I was fast-tracking to become the first female manager in Sun Life. At Heathrow, going through security when you walk through a door-frame to see if you're carrying any metal, this lady kept setting off the machine. They frisked her couple of times but couldn't find anything. Eventually it turned out that she was wearing a wired bra. She never did become the first female manager. She was married to a colleague in the marketing department but took up with one of Sun Life's barristers and left. Today, a quarter of a century later, they're still together, happily married.

Sun Life held an annual management conference where all head office managers and sales branch managers and their wives spent three days and two nights together. Initially it was held in Bristol but they soon ventured to exotic places such as Coventry and Southampton. A bit of training, a bit of socialisation was what we saw in it. For the directors, who also attended, it was an opportunity to assess potential future directors. I'm OK at set piece events like a talk or a speech but hopeless at small talk and of course I can't dance. One year the Chairman's wife, probably a nice lady but one who talked like Hyacinth Bouquet, asked me for a dance. I didn't want to tread on her toes but didn't want to be rude to her either. Then I remembered that Brim Avery and I had messed about on the lawns pretending to play cricket. That gave me an idea. I said to her. 'You must excuse me. I'm a little stiff from bowling.' She looked at me contemptuously and said, 'So that's where you come from.'

I was now quite busy, designing products, getting the concept approved and then selling it to our own salesmen so that they may sell it to brokers. So I used to go home tired wanting to put my feet up. The kids of course wanted to see me and tell all about their day. Living close to my office meant that I couldn't make the transition from actuary to father. So I started staying behind for half an hour, perhaps reading *The Times*.

The kids believed in Father Christmas and were quite uninhibited in their demands of him. One day when I came home I sat in the TV room and asked Zamin to go upstairs and get my slippers from my wardrobe. Dutifully he went up and opened the wardrobe and there, awaiting wrapping, were all the Christmas presents. He was devastated. He could no longer ask for the earth as he knew that my resources were finite. Deena claimed that she already knew it was me but went along with the deception; apparently the letters that Father Christmas wrote to her were in my handwriting.

I didn't get to a cricket ground very often. But there was always television and John Woodcock in *The Times*. In 1984 the West Indies toured England again, but I saw no game. Gower was now captain and had a tough baptism as the series was lost five-nil. I have two outstanding memories of the 1984 summer. The first was a one-day international when England managed to get most of the team out for next to nothing, but Viv Richards scored a destructive 189 and had a last wicket stand of 106 of which Michael Holding scored twelve. He should have been charged with assault and battery. The other was of Fred Trueman, now in his dotage. A Test had ended early and I was doing the usual thing, watching the game on television with the sound on mute and listening to Test Match Special on radio. Fred was lamenting, 'I just don't know what's going on out there. There are no fast bowlers anymore. I retired years ago but I reckon I can still bowl faster than this lot.' Bear in mind that the English bowling attack included Bob Willis and Ian Botham. At this point they were showing on television the highlights of the famous Lord's Test of 1963, the one in which Cowdrey came in as last man with a broken arm. Fred opened the bowling and Conrad Hunte hit his first three balls for four. They must have a television monitor in the commentary box and Fred must have seen this as he stopped mid-sentence and said, 'Funny how black and white slows you down.'

Gower remained captain for the tour to India that winter. He was in no sort of form and the tour nearly got sabotaged by the assassination of Mrs Gandhi. However, the players remained and in the end played some exciting cricket. Gatting at last came good and Fowler scored stacks of runs. India got beaten although they discovered a new star in Azharuddin who scored a century in each of his first three Tests. Players who were on that tour described it as the happiest they'd been involved in. Neither Gooch nor Botham toured – I'm not implying anything I hasten to add.

Next summer Alan Border brought an Australian team to England and Gower had the best season of his career. Not only, as captain, did he win back the Ashes, but he scored a mountain of runs. Paradise, Elysium, Firdous, Nirvana, it surely cannot be better than England in 1985, the sun shining and Gower caressing balls in all direction. But the seeds of his downfall were planted by Gower himself. He had a slightly flippant nature and a line in humour which was characteristically English and capable of being misconstrued by the more literal minded. When after winning the Ashes he was asked about England's prospects in the forthcoming tour of the West Indies, he said tongue in cheek, 'I bet they are quaking in their shoes.' He should have known better. Viv Richards would never see the irony in that. Predictably they slaughtered England 5–0. When they returned to England, India beat them in the first Test.

Gower was replaced as captain by Gatting, who then remained captain for the tour to Australia. England started so badly that Martin Johnson coined the memorable phrase, 'There's only three things wrong with the England cricket team: can't bat, can't bowl, can't field'. But they came good and it was a harmonious tour. Botham was as good as gold. Gatting asked him to take charge of the young fast bowlers and he took Defrietas and Small under his wing. Gower, Lamb and Gatting got runs as did Botham. Botham also got his last five-for in Tests, bowling tripe. And there was a new star: Chris Broad.

England really should have been the second best team in the 1980s but they were a poor third. The whole never added up to the sum of its parts. Given the esteem in which Gooch is now held, it is interesting to reflect how minimal his contribution was in the eighties. He shone in the 1985 Ashes series, but Gower, Gatting and Robinson were brighter. He was completely neutered by Alderman in 1981 and 1989 and by the West Indies in 1984 and, of course, he took time out to make unofficial tours of South Africa.

What about Pakistan? It took Imran two years to recover from his injury and when he did, he was never the same bowler again as the out-swinger had gone. He played initially as a batsman only and then gingerly returned to bowling. In 1986 a series against the West Indies got his competitive juices flowing again. In the first Test, he and Qadir bowled out the West Indies for fifty-three to record a famous win. Mind you, they're not the world's top team without pride. They came back with a vengeance in the second Test, Malcolm Marshall being in top form. They had Pakistan on its knees in the third decider but Imran at his most dour batted out time.

Next, in 1986/7 was another frontier to cross. Could Pakistan be successful in India where they had failed in 1952/3, 1960/61 and 1979/80? As usual, it was a turgid series with neither side prepared to take risks and they got to the fifth Test with the series still standing at 0–0. The Indian authorities were clearly scared of Pakistan's speed attack of Imran Khan and Wasim Akram and had prepared dead pitches. For the final Test in Bangalore, there was pressure to prepare a 'results' pitch. India picked three spinners, with Kapil Dev and Roger Binny to provide the faster stuff. This suggested that they expected a turner.

Pakistan must have expected a seaming surface as they picked three seamers and two spinners. Imran in his *All Round View* says that he chose to replace Abdul Qadir with Iqbal Qasim. That may have been factually and chronologically correct, but Miandad in his autobiography, *Cutting Edge,* said that he had to almost get on his hands and knees to get Imran to pick Qasim. Either way Qasim played.

Pakistan batted first and were dismissed for 116, batsman after batsman falling to attacking strokes. Maninder Singh picked up seven wickets for twenty-seven. When India batted, Dilip Vengsarkar scored a disciplined fifty and India overtook Pakistan with only four wickets down. His departure saw Pakistan stage a strong comeback, so that the eventual lead was a mere twenty-nine. Iqbal Qasim and Tauseef Ahmed shared the wickets equally. Javed Miandad was sent in to open with Ramiz Raja and they cleared the deficit. The top order batted with greater discipline than in the first innings. Everyone chipped in and

India were left a target of 221. Time was not an issue.

Wasim got Pakistan off to a great start by dismissing Kris Srikanth and Mohinder Amarnath off successive deliveries. After that, the spinners took over. They steadily worked their way through the batting line up, all except Sunil Gavaskar, who was playing one of his best innings, fit to rank with his 221 at the Oval in 1979 or the century in Manchester in 1974. The ball was turning square, bouncing most of the time but on occasions keeping low. It was riveting stuff. Eventually Gavaskar fell for ninety-six and Pakistan won by sixteen runs. Imran did not bowl in the second innings but had achieved, perhaps, Pakistan's greatest win since the Oval in 1954. There followed a tour of England.

I organised a party from work to go to the Oval to watch a one-day International between England and Pakistan. It was in May and it was relatively warm when we set out in a coach from Bristol at a quarter to eight. In the bright open spaces of Kennington it was pretty cold and all of us shivered all day. My recollection is of a dull, one-sided match, but Wisden suggests that it was closer than that, England reaching the target with eleven balls to spare. Imran was now thirty-four and assumed a low-key patriarchal role, letting his manager Haseeb Ahsan do all the talking and, boy, he liked his own voice. He had an axe to grind against the English.

A quarter of a century earlier he had been a star bowler, a sort of right-handed Underwood in that he bowled medium-paced spinners, though not with Derek Underwood's accuracy but with more spin. He'd been a surprise pick for the tour to West Indies in 1957/8 and played an important role in the win in the fifth Test. He then toured India in 1960/61 and took six for 202 from eighty-four overs in the fourth Test in Madras. He was picked as key member of the bowling attack for the 1962 tour of England under Javed Burki. Very early in the tour umpires queried his action. Burki did not dissent or challenge them, but sent Haseeb home and a promising career was ended.

Haseeb played in the Karachi Test (in 1961/62) in which Dexter score a double hundred. My naked eye couldn't detect anything but equally I wasn't looking for anything. On the 1987 tour Haseeb seemed to revel in causing mayhem. Even though Pakistan won the series 1–0, I didn't enjoy the tour. It wasn't played in the right spirit. It was with this tour that I started falling out of love with Pakistan cricket.

The role of Imran in shaping Pakistan's cricket can never be overestimated. He introduced discipline in the Pakistan team, sorted out internecine warfare and overcame the fear of failure. Pakistan drew three successive series against the West Indies and could legitimately claim to be the second best team in the world. It wasn't the best collection of players Pakistan have fielded. That accolade must go to either the 1976/7 side that toured West Indies under Mushtaq or the 1996 side led by Wasim Akram that played England. But the 1987 team was more combative and had better results against top teams. Imran got rid of the inferiority complex that had blighted previous teams. However, there was an unfortunate consequence of this. Aggression on the field of play often crossed the line beyond which lay cheating. Salim Yusuf claimed a catch off a bumped ball at Headingley in 1987; Miandad did the same in the third Test of 1982 when fielding at slip.

The World Cup was played on the Indian sub-continent the following winter and it was widely predicted that it would be an India–Pakistan final. In the event, both fell in the semi-final. Imran miscounted the sequence of bowlers towards the end of the Australian innings, leaving Salim Jaffer, his weakest bowler, to bowl the final over. Earlier Salim Jaffer had bowled five expensive overs for thirty-nine. Now Steve Waugh took seventeen off the final over, one fewer than the final margin of victory. England beat India in the other semi, Gooch scoring a masterly 115, relying almost exclusively on the sweep shot. It was a close final between England and Australia, the latter winning by seven runs and thereby kick-starting their twenty-year-long renaissance. Everyone blamed the defeat on Mike Gatting's reverse sweep that led to his downfall. Wonderful thing, hindsight.

England toured Pakistan immediately afterwards, the tour famous for the 'Shakoor Rana incident'. In defence of Gatting, it has to be said that, as is often the case, he blew his top on the wrong issue. Poor umpiring had dogged them and caused extreme frustration. Some of it was not poor umpiring, but different umpiring; a greater willingness to give lbw to flippers. But there were errors as well.

Once the dispute happened, Miandad allegedly orchestrated the response in much the same way as Kardar did in the ragging incident way back in 1955. Not a nice man. Imran called him a street-fighter.

He was certainly not one for the diplomatic corp. The controversy was milked for all its worth by the tabloids. A lot of old cricketers joined in. 'They've been robbing us for years,' said Tom Graveney. Tom was censured for speaking his mind. The quality of umpiring in Pakistan has been an issue for over fifty years; for as long as the country has been in existence in fact.

It is worth examining the issues briefly. There are three possible reasons for poor umpiring: the umpires could be incompetent; or there may be home team bias; or, it could be that the tourists suffer from paranoia. Let us consider each in turn.

There were good reasons for Pakistani umpires to be incompetent in the past. There was no formal system of coaching or regulation of umpires and no way of knowing whether they were fully conversant with the laws of the game. It seemed sufficient that they had played first-class cricket; sufficient, but not necessary. Nor did they get sufficient practice as umpires as there were too few first-class matches. In the circumstances, it is surprising that they were not all incompetent. Players can live with incompetence, even if errors seldom even out over a match.

Bias is a different matter. Tom Graveney smelt bias in 1951/52, Tony Lock, Ken Barrington and Fred Titmus in 1955 and most famously, Sobers in 1959. Sobers was so incensed at the spate of lbw decisions Fazal Mahmood won at his expense that he nearly went home. Two decades later, Kim Hughes in 1982 and Sunil Gavaskar (1982/3) were both unhappy and, now, so were Mike Gatting and his entire team. In every case Pakistan vehemently denied bias and suggested that, if there were errors, it was due to human fallibility. Most of the time, they attributed it to paranoia and distrust of alien conditions.

It is true that visiting players can develop a siege mentality in Pakistan. Climate, food, people are all alien and the lack of entertainment contributes to a sense of futility. But there must be an underlying concern about bad umpiring for it to develop paranoia. Every bad decision can then seem to be bias. The reactions of Indian tourists should be a good guide as they're least likely to find the conditions alien. In a later chapter ('Shattered Dreams') I give Lala Amarnath's views on umpiring. Here I would like to refer to the experience of Gulab Ramchand who toured Pakistan in 1954/55.

He was brought up in Karachi and in fact went to St Patrick's, the school I studied in. He therefore had enormous affection for the place. In an article in the Chennai daily, *The Hindu*, a high quality paper, he said that when they toured smaller cities such as Lyallpur and Montgomery (now Sahiwal and Faisalabad) the tourists were not put up in hotels or even people's homes. They had to sleep in the railway sidings at the station. They had to wash and bathe there too and found their faces black with soot afterwards. When they went to bigger cities such as Bahawalpur, where they played a Test match, all the good quality accommodation was given to Pakistani dignitaries and the touring players had to stay with families in very poor accommodation. Mind you, Ramchand also had a go at the Indian Control Board for making Indian Test players travel third class when he was captain, whereas the Aussie tourists travelled air-conditioned first class in the same train. Maybe it is the general tightfistedness of administrators. Ian Chappell said the same of Don Bradman, the administrator, although only after the Don was safely dead.

At the time of the Shakoor Rana incident, I had no strong view one way or the other. I knew Miandad was a needler and someone who would be prepared to go beyond the limits of fair play in the interests of a win; but I also felt that Broad and Gatting might see provocation where none was intended.

Players remember decisions that have gone against them, but forget ones they've benefited from. Don Bradman (*Farewell to Cricket*) claimed that at the Oval in 1930, the umpire wrongly gave him out caught behind off Larwood for 232. As evidence, he shows a photograph with a very docile-looking George Duckworth; Duckworth was usually a raucous appealer. Don was trying to discredit Larwood's thesis that the origin of bodyline lay in Bradman's discomfort against fast, short-pitched bowling in that match. In Duncan Hamilton's recent biography of Harold Larwood (*Harold Larwood*), Harold makes no reference to this, but alleges that in the Third Test, when Bradman scored 334, he should have been out first ball, when he snicked Larwood to the wicket-keeper, Duckworth. It is likely that both Bradman and Larwood were right.

In 1990/91 Pakistan were the first to stage a home Test series with neutral umpires. Gradually it became the norm. Today there are two Pakistani umpires on the elite panel, Aleem Dar and Asad Rauf; indeed Aleem Dar has just been voted the top umpire for the third year running.

The recently retired Imran was persuaded to return. The prospect of playing the West Indies in the Caribbean was a sufficient carrot. His bowling and a century from Miandad helped win the first Test, but Marshall won the second Test. The third was drawn but poor umpiring saved the home team.

Meanwhile, changes were afoot on the work front and it looked as if my star was on the wane. Luckily I was approached by a head hunter to join Royal Life Insurance based in Liverpool. The carrot was the prospect in the near future of becoming its Actuary, something I was unlikely to achieve at Sun Life where I had focussed on the marketing side of the business. I consulted the family first as they were well settled. All three said 'Go for it,' bless them, so I accepted the offer and by the year end I had bid farewell to a lot of good friends.

Just so that there is no misunderstanding, if my star was on the wane, it must have been partly my own doing. I was a one-off, too given to pranks. One that backfired took place in 1986. We were planning a driving holiday in Tuscany and Brim Avery started winding me up mercilessly. 'You'll never get there or if you do you'll never get back.'

So I decided to play a prank. Before I left for the holiday I sat down and composed a carefully crafted letter and wrote it out in neat steady hand. I said that I'd got lost on the Parisian peripherique, went the wrong way round it and had a nasty accident. The car, a company car was a write-off, and so and so forth. The letter was the work of a cool, rational mind, not that of someone who'd been through a nasty accident. I was convinced that they'd see it as a joke, not least because I'd sent it to Brim, not to my boss Peter Pummell. Brim did not open the letter. Instead it was opened by the Director of Administration, a small-minded man promoted way beyond his competence. He would routinely open other people's mail and he opened my letter and read it. He panicked and thought of sending a search party. He talked to Peter who read my letter and saw it for what it was. When I came back he did say, 'It's done your career no good at all.'

I was to discover a couple of years later, my family didn't want to move and had said 'Yes' because they thought that was what I wanted. They were very unhappy on the Wirral. When I realised this I agreed that we would aim to move back south as soon as Zamin and Deena were at University as it did not make sense to uproot them yet again.

13. 1988–1991

A t Royal, I was to report to Jeff Medlock, who had played cricket against Clive Lloyd and Harry Pilling. When I moved to the Wirral he invited me over for dinner. There, to my surprise, was a collection of Wisdens in a dedicated bookshelf. And not just a few like mine, but a complete set. It turned out that his father, Ken, had at one stage been the Chairman of John Wisden Ltd, the sports goods manufacturer who also published the Almanack. You can see him in the 1964 edition, occupying a central position and beaming in the photograph of the presentation of the Wisden Trophy to Frank Worrell. Jeff's son Jonathan is also an avid collector of Wisdens.

One of the young actuaries who reported to me in Royal was Chris O'Brien, a cricket fan, who told me that he was a founder member of the Lancashire County Cricket Club, which was formed in the nineteenth century whereas he was born in 1951. Founder member is a category of members which is fixed in number. At the outset they were the people who founded the club. Those that died or resigned were replaced by the same number of new members.

Bill Scanlan was the Chief Executive of Royal Life, a tall man with a slight stoop and a purposeless lope reminiscent of Gary Cooper, but with a sharp-shooting mind rather than a gun. He treated every business challenge as an intellectual problem to be solved, which he would and arrive at a decision which involved someone else, usually one of his directors, implementing it. He would then pass the file to him and expect it to be dealt with.

There was a lot going on at Royal and I was too busy finding my feet. To compound matters, I was elected to the Council of the Institute of Actuaries in 1988. I was therefore unable to follow cricket seriously in 1988 and 1989.

Royal Life was a major player in the mortgage market. Its Sales

Director, David Parry claims to have invented the mortgage endowment although it might be like the discovery of calculus, others might have done it concurrently. Royal had close ties with building societies but these were under threat as the Financial Services Act came into effect in April 1988. Societies that purported to be independent would have to recommend the best product, which was unlikely to be ours. They could however tie to a single company and sell its products alone and that was the route we were pursuing. This was David Parry's main task in 1988, cajoling societies to tie to us. Such decisions are made on commercial logic, but it helps if you get on well socially. So a series of friendly football matches were arranged.

We had a guy in our admin department, the gentlest of souls at work but once he'd got his football gear on he made Roy Keane look like Mother Theresa. In one such game, three of the opponent's players had to be stretchered off with broken legs, carried off to be more precise, there being no stretchers. David Parry was furious,

'You'll pay for this. This is a friendly. You're supposed to let them win without making it obvious, not break their legs.'

'I know, David, but he started it.'

'Who did? I didn't see anything?'

'Their centre half fouled me. It was vicious.'

'I didn't see that. When did it happen and how come the ref and I both missed it?'

'It happened last year, when I was playing for Heswall against Crewe.'

There may or may not be a connection but the society went elsewhere with their business.

A settled team, a settled captain, there was cautious optimism when the West Indies arrived in the summer of 1988. 'We should be able to draw at least one Test.' Well, after the first Test, Gatting was caught with a hotel maid. Although he protested that 'nothing happened' (it wasn't clear whether that was a statement of fact or an expression of regret), he got the sack anyway. Embury captained in the next two Tests and then, out of nowhere, Chris Cowdrey was appointed captain for the fourth Test. Although the press was fiercely critical, he got it on merit. He was the godson of the Chairman of the selectors, Peter May. Finally they made Graham Gooch the captain. He was the best English batsman during the series.

Looking back, the initial optimism wasn't misplaced; we did manage to draw one Test. For the first time in a decade we had a home series without Botham. No new players were discovered. The West Indies side had several changes; Clive Lloyd, Michael Holding and Joel Garner had gone. Viv Richards was the captain and Curtly Ambrose was a new name. The star of the series was Malcolm Marshall.

The use of 'we' might surprise people who think I support only Pakistan. I'm reminded of the story about three friends, an actuary, an accountant and a lawyer discussing whether it was better to have a wife or a mistress.

'A wife is much better,' said the accountant. 'You can claim the married man's allowance for tax purposes.'

'No, a mistress is much better,' said the lawyer.' You avoid the cost of divorce.'

'No, no, it's best to have a wife and a mistress,' said the actuary.

'Why?' asked the other two.

'Because you can tell your wife, you're with your mistress and tell your mistress you're with your wife. That way you can stay at the office and work.'

Pakistan cricket might be my first love, but English cricket was a demanding mistress. In any case, as I indicated in the previous chapter, I was beginning to fall out of love with Pakistan cricket. This was something that was masked during the 90s by my passion for Wasim Akram and Saeed Anwar, two of my all-time favourite cricketers.

Inevitably there was a price to pay for England's failure. Peter May resigned and was replaced by Ted Dexter. Mickey Stewart was the team manager and it was announced that David Gower was reinstated captain. This surprised many. We discovered later that Mickey Stewart didn't want to be anywhere near Gower. But Dexter didn't want Graham Gooch, the incumbent; he wanted Gower back. Dexter won, which was a pity, as it is tough for a captain to work with a manager who doesn't want him. Much as I admire Gower the batsman and fielder and Gower the man, he is no captain. No man who will not use one word where ten would do, can make a rousing motivational speech whether of the 'cornered tigers' type or 'Once more unto the breach, dear friends' variety. Like me, he'd try to find flippant humour where the situation demanded gravity. It probably shortened his playing career. I know, as my flippancy did my career no good either.

England were thrashed.

Royal had operations worldwide and in 1988 we organised an international conference of actuaries in a hotel in Yorkshire. It was a week-long affair and on the last night we organised a dinner in a Michelin-rated restaurant called the Real McCoy. We organised this six months in advance and then realised that it clashed with a World Cup semi-final. We didn't think that England would make it to the semi and as the Yanks and the Strines did not do football, we let it stand. In the event, England did well and Sod's Law being what it is, their key game against Germany fell on that night. It was too late to rearrange the dinner. Instead, we got our hotel to record the match and made the restaurant promise a news blackout. We finished our excellent meal with indecent haste and rushed back to the hotel.

'Yes Sir, we've taped it for you,' said the head barman. Whilst the rest of us got our orders in, he switched the video-recorder on. All he got was a sandstorm.

'Oh no,' said a chorus of voices.

'I've definitely taped it,' he said struggling to replace the sandstorm with a picture. Eventually he gave the television a kick and suddenly a picture appeared. It was in black and white. He kicked it again. Back came the sandstorm,

'What did you do that for?' we asked.

He kicked it again and the picture returned; in black and white.

'Leave it, leave it.'

'Yes, leave it. We'll pretend it's the 1966 final,' said another England supporter.

The barman left us with the parting words, 'Shame the result is different.' How he escaped lynching, heaven only knows.

Shortly after I joined, Royal Life recruited an Irish chartered accountant as the Finance Director. He was, I was told, a gold medallist having topped in his accountancy exams. He may have been a brilliant accountant but he had no people skills. He was based in Peterborough and most of us were in Liverpool. He would arrange a meeting for 9 am, knowing full well that the only way the Liverpool crowd could make it was by setting off at 5 am driving north and then across east and then south along the M1. He was the boss, so we accepted it. We'd all be there on time and wait for him. There would be no sign of him. At 9.15 he would look in, not say anything, but disappear. Eventually he'd turn up an hour late, not having done any preparation. He'd start reading the papers whilst we twiddled our thumbs. He also did something no manager should do: publicly humiliate his No. 2. This happened every time. Eventually the Board had to sack him or, to quote the official announcement, 'After completing a special assignment for the Managing Director, he will leave to pursue other interests.' He obviously was not a politician or he would have left to spend more time with his family.

The 1989 series against Australia was a nadir for England, made worse by the fact that Australia appeared to have found a winning formula. In their despair, the selectors turned to Graham Gooch for the winter's tour of the West Indies and left Gower out of the squad. The man who missed tours because he wanted to be with his wife, the man who courted the apartheid rand because he wanted to provide for his wife, now returned as a Malvolio type of character. Rigorous training and hard work was in and fun was out. In due course he was to acquire a new hair piece and a new wife. He famously clashed with Gower, whose *laissez-faire* approach he thought was a bad example.

Gower was recalled for the tour to Australia the following winter. Although not a devotee of the Gooch/Stewart training regime, his cricket continued to be of a high standard. He scored top in each of the first Three Tests, with centuries in the second and third. However, he did not help himself with his off the field antics: the Tiger Moth incident.

Then, in the fourth Test, a seemingly lazy waft to a leg-side delivery cost Gower his wicket just before lunch. Gooch saw red and Gower could not buy a run in the remainder of the series. He was dropped again, but had to be recalled to counter Wasim and Waqar. He handled their reverse swing as well as anybody and saw off a ferocious spell of theirs to see England to victory at Headingley. But he was not picked for the tour India the following winter or against Australia the following year. He hung on, hoping that the new captain Atherton might select him for the Caribbean tour. He did not, preferring to go for youth. Many people have likened him to Majid Khan. Both relied heavily on hand–eye coordination and timing but had limited footwork. Such players are more vulnerable when age slows down reflexes although there was little evidence of this in Gower.

That the animosity was personal, rather than driven by cricketing considerations, is demonstrated by the fact that Gooch brought Botham back into the team, well past his sell-by date and a far worse hedonist than Gower; and Gatting, rotund Gatting. To be fair to Gooch, he did get England to the final of the 1992 World Cup and they were the best team in the tournament. Botham has since said that that excessive training had meant that they were burnt out by the time they got to the final.

Gooch's own batting blossomed and he played some magnificent innings, notably the centuries at Leeds against the West Indies (1991) and Pakistan (1992) on bowler-friendly pitches. Statistically he had a Bradmanesque series against India in 1990 when he scored a triple century and century at Lords.

It was in April 1990 that Norman Tebbit[1] introduced the concept of the Tebbit Test. In an interview he said:

'A large proportion of Britain's Asian population fail to pass the cricket test. Which side do they cheer for? It's an interesting test. Are you still harking back to where you came from or where you are?'

As is often the case, the proposition has been hijacked. However it's worth reflection. I totally agree that an immigrant who has taken up residence and citizenship should assimilate into society and strive to make the host nation prosperous. This is not to say that they should totally lose their identity. British society is not homogeneous.

Having said all that, I am not sure that your allegiance at sport is necessarily an indication of your political, emotional or economic loyalties. Look at the support for Manchester United from people who've never set foot on this island. Sporting loyalties formed in one's youth never change. If you grew up a supporter of Arsenal you'd remain one, even if you spend all your adult life in Australia or the US. What confuses the issue is that, whilst in football you support your club rather

---

1.   Now Lord Tebbit

than your country, in cricket it is the country's team that you support. It is therefore easy to assume that an immigrant cricket supporter is disloyal. I follow Pakistan cricket team, but care not a fig about their hockey team or their squash players. I support the England cricket team too. In fact I got a greater thrill out of the Ashes win of 2005 than Pakistan's World Cup win of 1992.

That is the case for the defence of immigrants whose sporting loyalties were formed abroad. It does not explain why kids born in this country choose not to support England. I cannot condone them or their sometimes provocative behaviour.

It was strange, following cricket whilst working in Liverpool. Scousers were sports mad and would follow all sport, but there was no doubt that football was their true passion. Actuarial students found it harder to find time to study with so many games to watch; although it was hardest for Ray Curry who, being a Reading supporter, had to travel every weekend as even home matches were in effect away. In the end he had to choose between an actuarial career and one watching football. He chose the latter.

Two of the brightest people in Royal were two Oxbridge graduates, John Armstrong and Dave Williams. Both came as actuarial students. John's passion was bridge and Dave's football; John played (for England), Dave just watched. John was one subject away from qualifying as an actuary when he took stock and decided to quit exams. He feared that once he qualified he'd be promoted into management and office work would encroach upon bridge time. So he moved into IT and did a technical job on a strictly 9 to 5 basis, basically to feed himself and provide funds for his trips to bridge internationals. There was no money in bridge. Sadly, he died recently.

Dave was slightly different. He became an actuary and then decided to become an accountant and moved into the Finance area as he saw greater future there. He watched every football match Liverpool played in, home or away including European fixtures. (He was in Heysel stadium on the fateful day.) He had a bright man's gift of getting to the gist of the problem very quickly and explaining it very simply. He never appeared to have a difficult problem. In that he was a bit like David

Gower, making batting and fielding look so easy. Like Gower he was accused of being lazy when in fact he was far better than practically all accountants I saw at Royal. He hit a glass ceiling he had helped to erect. But he was a contented man.

Although there were a few colleagues who were not nice people, the team that worked for me, whether in Actuarial or Marketing or in our offshore company were all nice people. There was a good team spirit and when I eventually moved on I was sorry to leave them.

Around 1980, Glasgow was as run down as Liverpool, but the people of Glasgow and its local politicians got together and sorted the issues out. By the early nineties it was a re-born city. Liverpool on the other hand was left-wing dominated and whilst there were jobs available in the financial services sector, out-of-work dockers would not train for it. 'They're not jobs for men, they're for women and poofs.' They were natural wits and extremely funny but the humour had a bite to it. And their passion for Liverpool football Club had a religious fervour to it. I came to the conclusion that for the city to progress, the fortunes of its football club must decline.

Today, a quarter of a century later, we're getting there.

My mother-in-law visited us in the summer of 1991 and spent two or three happy months with us. She was still around when Zamin went to Trinity College, Cambridge, to read Maths. Seeing her joy, I wished that my father had lived to see it. He would have been a proud man.

Zamin is far brighter than I am and it is a matter of regret to me that he ruled out an actuarial career. Whilst he was doing 'A' levels, he spent one summer working in the Actuarial Department of the Royal where he came under the wing of Spencer Leigh, an actuary who specialised in underwriting. He was incidentally a very popular disk jockey on local radio and a fount of pop trivia knowledge. Spencer set the batch of school kids a project to review the published material on the impact of AIDS on life insurance. That was meat and drink to Zamin and he produced an excellent ten-page report. Spencer must have been impressed but his opening remark was, 'Did your Dad help you with the assignment?'

That finished it for him.

14. 1992–1996

The nineties was a period of transition for the insurance industry; when it was payback time for the excesses of the eighties. The old paternalistic attitude to customers was no longer acceptable. That undermined the bedrock of traditional life insurance, which is based on averaging. Averaging inevitably means that there are winners and losers. If retrospectively, the losers are compensated but the winners get to keep their gains, then the concept becomes unviable.

The cause of consumers was taken up by personal finance journalists, who in the main were women. In fact they made the genre the force it has become. I asked one of them how that happened. Apparently, in the seventies when women dared to enter the male preserve of hard drinking journalism, they were asked to report on births and deaths and fêtes. When they wanted something more challenging, they were asked to follow up marketing material issued by banks and insurance companies. The genre grew from there.

As Actuary, a bigger problem than the rise of consumerism was the fallout from the conquest of inflation. It had all sorts of consequences that were counter-intuitive. I had a tough time as a regular bringer of bad news to my Board. Fascinating though the issues were, they're outside the scope of this book.

In the spring of 1992, I became a director of Royal Life Insurance and the first thing we did was to carry out a major retrenchment programme which involved making several people who were personal friends redundant. In the business world your competitors do not down tools and wait for you to complete your re-organisation. They try to capitalise on your weakness so you cannot let up. Consequently 1992 and 1993 were the busiest years of my life. My focus didn't change but its intensity did. Work was still the primary focus but whilst in the eighties, family and cricket came joint second, from now on they came a distant fourth and there was nothing in the second and third place.

In 1994 Deena went to UCL in London to study French. It was a four-year course, one of which she had to spend in Paris. It was a wrench to see her go. I could write pages and pages about her but they fall outside the scope of this book. As this is the book about the life of a cricket fan I've made only passing reference to my family even though they're more important to me than anything else.

Royal Life had some rogue salesmen and we had to deal with the grievances of their customers. These were time-consuming tasks and, although we tried to be fair to the customers, they did not always see it that way. One day we found that details of confidential discussions between the Directors was being reproduced in the trade press. With a journalistic spin put on the story we were coming out in a bad light. Some of the internal memos, particularly from me, used unguarded language. One of the general management team or his secretary had to be the source of the leak so trust was broken down. Until we traced the source of the leak, it paralysed decision-making and we stopped discussing anything at all contentious.

We eventually located the source of the leak. We sacked him and issued an injunction asking him to return all company documents in his possession. That amounted to three or four crate-loads. He'd taken copies of all juicy or potentially incriminating documents.

We wasted a lot of time precisely when time was scarce. Both I and the Finance Director, David Heather, were extremely busy. We had more decisions to make than there was time available to do them justice and decisions had to be made on poor quality information. So it was a case of going for the least worst set of decisions.

David incidentally was built like Billy Bunter but in his prime was a top quality sportsman. Not only did he play rugby to a good standard, but he also did the 4x100m hurdles. At one stage or the other in his career he had raced against all four members of the British 4x100m hurdles quartet at the 1960 Olympics. At the time of the Mexico Olympics, he was keen to watch David Hemery in the 4x400m hurdles final but his wife had gone into labour. He returned home after his son was born and at around 2 am switched on the radio just in time to catch the end of the race. A very hoarse David Coleman was saying, 'He's done it, Hemery's done it. He's won the gold for Britain, Hennige from West Germany is second and the third is, the third is, oh who cares about who's third.' But we did care, because it was Sherwood, another British runner. The following morning he heard it again on the news. They'd edited out the 'who cares' bit of commentary and recorded a fresh one.

Another colleague, who was the head of HR was Roger Greenway, an ugly golfer but the best in Royal with a low single-figure handicap. He was also a quality wicket-keeper batsman, good enough to play at Lord's for England Schools against a South African Schools team that contained Barry Richards and Mike Proctor. He tells me that he dropped Barry first ball. Richards went on to get a hundred.

David moved in 1993 to become the Finance Director of Royal's estate agency business. I had immense difficulty with his successor. That chap had an enormous ego and suffered from the not-invented-here-syndrome. He started with a negligible knowledge of life insurance accounting. Rather than trying to learn from others, he filibustered and slowed the business down. He started by looking at the previous year's 'DTI Returns' which contained pages and pages of tables of numbers. The last row had numbers which were rounded to the nearest integer and the last number in the last row was the total, also rounded to the nearest integer. Not surprisingly, the rounded total would often be one or two out compared to the total of the rounded individuals. (I might have lost the non-numerate reader at this point but believe me it's dead obvious. For example if there were two numbers each 1.51 their total would be 3.02 which would be rounded to 3. But each 1.51 would be rounded to 2 so that to the naked eye the total should be 4). He immediately concluded that actuaries cannot add.

It got to a stage where I would meet him in private and give him ideas that he could put forward as his own and get the glory. I was past caring about who got the credit and just wanted the job done; but he wouldn't accept them as they weren't his idea. The strange thing was that outside work I got on well with him and we went to a couple of cricket matches together. But boy, he was hard work at work. He believed in the old accountancy adage, 'If you look after the P&L, the balance sheet would take care of itself.' Well, that doesn't work with a life insurance company.

So, when Finance and Actuarial arranged a 'friendly' cricket match I decided to take part and sort the guy out; me at five foot two, trying to defeat a six foot four hunk with my medium-paced bowling. Kadeeja warned me not to play as I'd had no exercise of any sort for, well, years. But a man must do what a man must do.

Well, I measured my run up and moved rhythmically to the crease jumped or rather leapt into a sideways-on position, braced my right leg and, to the sound of a pistol shot, landed in a heap. I thought somebody had shot me with a rifle but nobody reacted. I got up, smiled, dusted myself and walked back to my mark. My knee didn't feel right but I commenced my run up again and again the same thing happened. This time I had difficulty standing up. My knee couldn't stand the weight. I was helped to my car and after a half-hour rest I went home and, on the following day I saw a physio. The knee is supported by ligaments which are a bit like the elastic in your brief. Once it loses its elasticity after stretching, it cannot go back to the original position. That is how my right knee is to this day. It's OK if I keep it vertical. The moment I apply sideways pressure the leg collapses. Perhaps it was punishment for not listening to Kadeeja.

The irony is that the Finance Director didn't play. He pulled out at the last minute. A small consolation came several years later, when we'd both left Royal. He was gracious enough to admit, when no one was hearing, that in every argument he had with me I was in the right and he was wrong, but for his own credibility he felt he couldn't give in.

Mind you, there were things I could have learned from him if I'd been alert. He was ruthless in not tolerating shoddy or inaccurate work from his staff. I was more tolerant and that on reflection was a mistake.

One day when I came back from lunch my secretary said, with a wink, 'There's a lady downstairs, wanting to see you. She doesn't want to see anyone else, only you.'

So I met her. Royal had an offshore company based in the Isle of Man that I was responsible for. It had its own management team that ran the business but the MD reported to me. It was important that decisions were made locally or the UK taxman would try to tax the company. This lady was a client of that company. She had a complaint and she was not satisfied with the way it had been dealt and in the end the MD said, 'Take it to Icki in Liverpool'. She was a Scandinavian .who had flown to Isle of Man and from there, came unannounced to see me in Liverpool. She had an investment of, from memory £55,000 and she was convinced that we were making a turn on the money without passing it on. Nothing would persuade her that we were not. She was very aggressive and loud. She had a squint in one eye and loudly burst into tears at the slightest perceived slight. She accused me of taking advantage of her 'because she was old and foreign and a woman.' In the end I said we clearly weren't going to reach a meeting of minds, I would suggest to the Isle of Man office to refund her money with interest. I asked her to tell me details of her Swedish bank account and we will deal with it speedily.

Suddenly, the tears disappeared, as did the hysterics and she said calmly, 'Oh, no I don't want the money back in Sweden; my taxman doesn't know about it.' She was all sweetness after it.

Another episode relating to our Isle of Man business is worth retelling. I was at Castletown airport waiting to catch a flight back to Liverpool, when I heard a voice say, 'Excuse me are you Mr Iqbal?'

I said, 'Yes,' and turned round. There standing was a most beautiful young women dressed in a business suit. She said,

'I've been longing to see you for a very long time.'

Not being used to pretty girls saying that to me, I was convinced that some practical joker was behind this. I looked round but couldn't see anyone I knew. The truth was more prosaic. She was a new sales consultant of ours who wanted some price concession on a big case. She'd been told that I was the abominable No-Man.

What happened to cricket whilst I was so pre-occupied? The Australian team was in the process of overtaking the West Indies as the top team in the world, although they did not achieve this until 1995. They achieved this under three completely different types of captain, Alan Border who turned the team around and started them on a winning streak; Mark Taylor who, without impairing the will to win instilled by Border, introduced a spark of inspiration; and Steve Waugh who killed off any residual hope the opposing team might have. But the fundamental reason for their success was the emergence of three all-time greats: Shane Warne, Glenn McGrath and, later, Adam Gilchrist; as well as a succession of world-class players: Boon, Jones, McDermott, Taylor, Slater, Mark and Steve Waugh, Gillespie and later, Hayden,

Langer and Martyn. It is true that their sledging went beyond the limits of acceptability – it was strange to hear Warne complain that Ranatunga of Sri Lanka sledged in a foreign language; stranger that Ranatunga shouldn't do it in English; what's the point in sledging, if the other bloke cannot understand it?

As to England, Graham Gooch continued to lead by example but without changing the team's fortune materially. Towards the end of the 1993 Ashes series he resigned and Mike Atherton took over. Mike started well and his batting actually improved. His was the wicket the opposition most wanted. When he took the team to the West Indies in 1993/94, in the first Test at Sabina Park, Courtney Walsh subjected him to forty minutes of sustained physical assault, there is no other word for it. To his credit, Atherton did not flinch. In the next Test, after being level pegging on the first innings, an inspired Curtly Ambrose pinned him lbw first ball and the whole team folded for forty-six. They hauled themselves off the floor and won the next Test, Alec Stewart scoring a hundred in each innings. Against South Africa in Johannesburg, he scored 185 not out, one of the greatest defensive innings ever.

He started promisingly as captain but was thwarted by two problems. The first was the lack of players of sufficient class. Indeed he had some problem players in Hick, Thorpe and Tuffnell who required careful handling. The second was the arrival of Ray Illingworth, who as manager, completely emasculated the captain of any authority. Atherton's chronic back condition got worse and in the end he probably carried on a year or two too long.

By 1992 Imran was nearing the end of his career and there was no visible sign of planning the succession. Javed Miandad, his locum, was also nearing the end. Ramiz Raja looked captaincy material but was not an automatic choice as a batsman. Wasim was an obvious candidate but was it was fair to saddle a fast bowling all-rounder with the burden of captaincy? Was Imran a prototype or a one-off?

Such thoughts were pushed to the back as the focus was on the 1992 World Cup. The tale of how Imran motivated a team that had such a disastrous run that it was on the brink of elimination, to go on to win is familiar to all; as is his 'cornered tigers' speech. What is overlooked is that they needed an extraordinary amount of luck, as their fate depended on the outcome of the matches they weren't involved in. Even in the final, had Gooch not dropped a fairly straightforward catch given by Imran,

Pakistan would not have built up a defendable total. Wasim Akram was the star of the final, settling the outcome with two magnificent deliveries that dismissed Lamb and Lewis.

At the time of the 1992 World Cup, external consultants we had retained were busy working on the retrenchment programme. They were staying in a hotel in Bebington on the Wirral which had Sky. They invited us to watch the final. A colleague Mel White and I went to join them. Play started around 3.30 am. Having been used to BBC's coverage I was impressed by the quality of Sky's coverage.

Imran forgot to thank his team in his acceptance speech and a rift appeared. He therefore chose to retire and Miandad captained the team that came to England in 1992.

Imran's legacy came in two parts. The first was the growth in interest in cricket following the successes of the eighties had brought forward a number of exciting players. The supply line seemed endless. The second was team harmony and unity. Different personalities had different objectives but they pulled together in a common cause. Alas he was unable to bequeath that. Javed by nature was a stirrer and confrontationist. Throughout the nineties, the Pakistan team was a bunch of outstanding individuals who were not pulling together as a team; rather like the Yorkshire cricket team of the fifties or Australia under the hapless Kim Hughes. No doubt the growth of match-fixing would have caused greater divisions between those in on it and those who were clean.

That said, 1992 was a very exciting series, the second, fourth and fifth Tests being particularly so. Time and again England would get to a position of comfort after the first 50–70 overs, only for reverse swing to take effect and the rest of the innings to fold up. There was much muttering about devious and illegal acts being committed upon the ball. In one match the ball was changed but the original ball disappeared from view suggesting a cover up by the authorities.

As we were to discover later, reverse swing works if one side is diligently polished but the other left to deteriorate. This requires the whole team to cooperate and often one player is nominated as the ball manager and the ball reaches the bowler via him. Wasim Akram, talking a decade later, said that they had to tick off Saqlain Mushtaq when, as the bowler, he tried to shine both sides.

Of course, the process of deterioration can be accelerated by using finger nails or even external aids: a penknife would be an obvious one, although no one has been accused of using one. However, in an attempt to deflect criticism from Wasim Akram and Waqar Younis, Imran Khan in an article in the *Telegraph* said that everyone tampers with the ball. Rather like driving speed limits, it was a question of degree. He said that once, and only once, he used a bottle top in a county match. All hell broke lose when the article was published. Players were careful of libel laws but off the record there was much muttering. How credible is it that he only used it once, unless it didn't work? We never got to the bottom of it, as Pakistan treated it as a slur on the nation rather than allow the facts to be reviewed objectively. To be fair to them, the reporting in the tabloids was provocative in the extreme.

Personally, like Mike Atherton, I'm in favour of legalising ball tampering. So much of the recent changes have been batsman friendly (heavier bats, shorter boundaries, flatter covered pitches) that it was high time something was done to redress the balance. Bowlers have always been the slaves or workhorses[1]. In the old days this could be seen very clearly; in the West Indies, where all the batsmen were white George Challenor, Karl Nunes, the Grant brothers and the fast bowlers black, John, Constantine, Martindale, Griffiths.

The 1992s one-day series had two games before and the remaining three after the thrilling Test series when England thrashed Pakistan. In the third and fourth games there were wides galore (eighteen and eleven). What surprised me was that Wasim, who in the Tests was landing yorkers with pin point accuracy, was all over the place. I thought he'd just lost his rhythm. I now wonder whether those matches were thrown, although no one has ever implicated Javed Miandad.

The following winter Miandad was replaced as captain by Wasim, with Waqar as vice-captain. Wasim could not make the transition from being one of the lads to the leader of the pack. It is suggested that he tried to cultivate the aloofness that was part of Imran's persona but in him it looked faked. It is also suggested that Waqar undermined him as he wanted the top job. Certainly the two, such a deadly combination as a bowling force, were never close although that is not uncommon. Think of Lock and Laker, Gough and Caddick, Bradman and anyone

---

1.   An exception is the greater willingness for umpires to give front-foot lbw decisions in the bowler's favour since the advent of Hawkeye.

else. Wasim was replaced by Salim Malik. When he got caught in a match-fixing scandal, almost everyone was tried as captain: Saeed Anwar, Ramiz Raja, Moin Khan, Amir Sohail, Rashid Latif. By the time the World Cup came round in 1995, Wasim was back in charge.

In 1994, Mark Taylor, newly appointed as captain of Australia, played a series in Pakistan led by Salim Malik. Taylor started with a pair in the first Test in Karachi and lost the Test they should have won when Inzamam and Mushtaq Ahmed put on fifty-eight for the last wicket. The winning runs came when Inzamam skipped down the pitch to Warne, missed the ball, but so did Healey and the ball went for four byes. The rest of the series was a batting triumph for Salim Malik but he will be remembered for something else. Shane Warne and Mark Waugh reported that he had offered them a substantial bribe to throw the match.

This was a slow-burning fuse that was only properly lit after the Indian police charged Hansie Cronje and, after early denial, he made a confession. Simon Wilde has written an excellent book, *Caught*, on the subject and I will be very brief. The Pakistan Cricket Board launched the Qayyum Enquiry which published a report that was extensive but in some respects unsatisfactory. Several players such as Inzamam, Mushtaq Ahmed, Saeed Anwar were criticised for not co-operating fully. Wasim Akram was recommended never to be made captain again. All bark and no bite; the only sanction to carry weight was the ban on Salim Malik. The problems that emerged a decade later arose from the PCB's failure to force players to co-operate fully with the Enquiry and also its failure to implement all of the recommendations, such as regular audit of the player's bank accounts. It placed short term success over long term good.

Wasim was reinstated as captain and he led a successful tour of England in 1996. Not only were they successful, there was harmony within the team and between the two sides. In his second coming Wasim struck the right balance between authoritativeness and chumminess. The series had magnificent batting by Saeed Anwar and Inzamamul Haq. Wasim did not have a great time with the ball but Mushtaq Ahmed and Waqar shone. A major new find was Saqlain Mushtaq, the inventor of the doosra but he could not get into the Test side.

I was in heaven, not because Pakistan won; I was fond of Mike Atherton and would have quite liked him to win. No, I had a new hero, Saeed Anwar. He was in the same mould as Majid Khan and David

Gower. He started his Test career with a King Pair against the West Indies and the selectors concluded that he was not fit for Test cricket. He was picked again after a long gap and had some excellent innings against Mark Taylor's Australians. I know that Shane Warne rates him. Apparently Glenn McGrath, who was a miser, hated him because even his defensive shots went for runs. He had wrists of steel and, in spite of the field square of the wicket on the off-side being packed with fielders, he obtained a large proportion of his runs in that region. Boy, was he good to watch. Unlike Majid and Gower, he was an ordinary fielder.

The Lord's Test was played against a background of a defamation case that was brought to the High Court against Imran by Botham. An article had appeared in the Indian press which quoted Imran as saying that ball-tampering was as old as the hills and many bowlers, even Botham, did it. Imran went to great lengths to avoid the matter reaching the courts. He was misquoted; he would never say that of Botham; he was prepared to publicly say that in the form of an article. Botham would have none of it. A pound of flesh was called for. Ian was badly advised as one can never be certain of the outcome when such a case goes to the courts. In the event he lost and was saddled with huge legal fees.

Zamin got a double first. It was a proud family that went to Cambridge to see him receive his degree in a ceremony conducted in Latin. He stayed on to do his masters.

Some time in the mid-nineties I had a letter from a Manchester-based Islamic organisation. They targeted affluent Muslims, using the electoral register. They were after funds and the letter ended with a chilling warning, 'If you don't support us don't be surprised if misfortune befalls a member of your family'; or words to that effect. There was no way I'd support them with that kind of threat. Yet I decided not to tell the police. Probably, I was wrong not to do so. I did not tell my family either. It hardened my resolve to move back south. I began to put out feelers to find another job to keep up my promise to my family to return south as soon as Zamin and Deena were at college.

15. 1997–2004

In 1996 an unexpected opportunity arose. Royal merged with Sun Alliance and the combined group had two sets of directors that needed to be thinned down to one set. I threw my hat in the ring saying, 'Please can I be one of those who leave?' So it was that by the end of 1996 I was back in London. Kadeeja and I decided to make our home in Cobham, Surrey, half a mile from Colin Coles and his wife Pat.

I joined Bacon & Woodrow, a firm of consulting actuaries. I suspect that I was hired because, within the insurance industry, I had extensive experience of marketing and was well known. Although I was usually marketing products designed by me, I marketed them as the *company's* products, which I could do with objective detachment. I found marketing Bacon & Woodrow much more difficult. This is because when you are a professional, whether an accountant, lawyer or actuary, you are really selling yourself. You're really saying, 'Look how good I am, come and use me.'

I marvelled at colleagues at Bacon and Woodrow, such as Tony Fine, Andrew Smith, Tim Sheldon, Duncan Ferguson, David Murray, Demos Papasavvas, Ian Clark, Steve Shurety, Rory O'Brien, all essentially modest people, who talked at great length of their personal achievements when in a sell mode. I couldn't do it. I accept that I had less to boast about, but I didn't make the most of what little I had. It was payback for a lifetime of self-deprecation.

As part of my duties at Bacon & Woodrow, I had to entertain clients and potential clients in corporate hospitality tents at Lord's and the Oval. I know it's a tough life but somebody has to do it. On the first such occasion, against Australia in 1997, it rained all day. Fred Trueman and other stars of the past made an appearance. I was standing next to a grey-haired gentleman in a business suit. I thought he was a client and made conversation with him. He started talking about Lillee and

Thomson and I joined in. I made conversation for a little while before I realised that something was amiss. He was obviously miffed that I didn't recognise him. When he dropped large hints I twigged that he was David Steele. In my defence I quoted some of his statistics but he corrected me when I got them slightly wrong.

In 1997 Sheena Carmichael gave a talk to the Institute of Actuaries on the subject of Business Ethics. She made a throwaway remark accusing the profession of discrimination against women and nonwhites, both of whom were under-represented in the actuarial profession. I had to speak up to deny the charge. I myself had never felt that discrimination had been an issue for me. Whilst it was true that Asians and women were under-represented, there were other reasons for it. The syllabus requires a good knowledge of maths, so most entrants have a maths degree. Until very recently, girls didn't go for maths degrees; nor did Asian boys. Asians prefer to be doctors and dentists. If you examine the ethnic mix of medical schools, Asians would be over-represented. Is that discrimination? I find the whole debate sterile. You are what you are. I'm a short, brown, Asian Muslim. And yet I've never been conscious of my ethnic or religious background when talking to say, a white Christian. Perhaps I'm conscious that I'm small, but otherwise I go by the personality and interests of the person.

Perhaps it's because I had an Anglophile father, perhaps it's because I've never been on the look out for slights, the truth is that in all my years in this country I've not sensed any discrimination against me, not at work, not in life. Banter, yes, but I had far worse in Pakistan. Sure, I've had my share of disappointments in my career, but I've usually found that I was to blame – perhaps I lacked the requisite political guile, perhaps I tend to be flippant when the situation demanded gravity, perhaps the other guy was better; yes, surprise surprise, that is possible for most of us.

This is in striking contrast to the belief of many Asians. Perhaps I'm lucky. But the irony is that discrimination is rife in India and Pakistan. It is an accepted part of the landscape; only it is known by its complement, favouritism. You don't discriminate against someone, you favour your own or others who're prepared to grease your palm. On the other hand, I would be surprised if any country in the world is as tolerant as the UK.

This is not to deny the existence of the BNP, or bribery and corruption, but we have to retain a sense of perspective.

Has multi-culturalism failed or has it worked? What answer do you want? What I do believe is that to try and retain your old culture without any cross-fertilisation, is a sure route to ossification. Those who oppose this quote a saying in Urdu, '*Dhobi ka kutta, na ghar ka na ghat ka,*' which translates as 'He who keeps his foot in both camps ends up being in neither'.

Progress comes only from learning from others. A lot of what Muslims regard as Muslim culture is really Arab culture which has nothing to with Islam. Islamic civilisation at its peak assimilated the knowledge of the Hindus, the Greeks, the Romans and the Persians. It had nothing to do with the religion; it was the natural curiosity of a number of outstanding intellects, who happened to be Muslims.

I also believe that the attempt to eradicate inequality (gender, race, sexual orientation) has run its course and some of the legislation should be peeled back. People should be able to compete on merit.

One day my colleagues in Bacon & Woodrow played a friendly cricket match against the colleagues from a different department. I did what I was least worst at, I umpired. The following year I was having drinks in our local with colleagues from work. A young Australian started talking to me as if he knew me.

'Do I know you?' I asked.

'You should do, I know you.'

'How do you know me?'

'Aren't you the bastard who gave me out caught behind by Steve Shurety last year?'

'Oh that was you was it? I suppose you think you didn't hit it?'

'Too bloody right.'

'I suppose you'll never forget it.'

'Too bloody right.'

An unexpected pleasure was an invitation to attend the wedding of Allen Kelly and Christine. I was able to catch up with several colleagues from the Northern days. Another was the opportunity to meet a childhood hero, Shujauddin. I adored him because, like me, he was small, batted right-handed and bowled left-handed and, being of limited skill was usually the last person to be picked for the team. He'd written *From Babes of Cricket to World Champion,* an excellent history of Pakistan cricket which was, unusually for a Pakistani cricket book, error and idiom-free. I wrote to congratulate him and that led to a meeting in his house in Hounslow, West London. He gave me four hours of his time and a candid account of his career. What struck me was his searing honesty, both in regard to himself and others. He clearly felt that his career was limited by Kardar, the captain being a similar cricketer. Yet he admitted that Kardar was a better batsman and fielder. I quote some of his views in the last chapter of this book.

In 1998 South Africa toured England. They had a long history of defensive captaincy going back to Dudley Nourse, Jackie McGlew and Trevor Goddard. Hansie Cronje was the same. Atherton had stepped down as captain and Alec Stewart had taken over. One Test South Africa should have won was drawn because Cronje declared too late and then Robert Croft masterminded a wonderful rearguard action. But the highlight of the series was the duel between Mike Atherton and Alan Donald. The latter bowled like a demon after Atherton gloved a catch and did not walk, he never does, and was given not out. The nearest I've seen to Donald's fury was from Mike Tyson in his early days as World Heavyweight Champion. Atherton won the duel but it was hair-raising stuff.

Immediately before the World Cup of 1999, Pakistan toured India and took part in an exciting series. The first Test at Chennai was a thrilling match dominated by Saqlain Mushtaq who took ten wickets, a young Shahid Afridi who made 141 and Sachin Tendulkar who played a masterly innings of 136 and took India close to victory. When he was out, the innings subsided and India lost by sixteen runs. Saqlain took another ten wickets in the second Test but Pakistan's batting failed and they lost by 212 runs. Anil Kumble became the first bowler, after Jim Laker, to take ten wickets in an innings. A bachelor (then) who lived with his mother, he joked after the match, that on the morning of every match his mother used to say, 'Take a hat-trick, take a hat-trick,' and from now on she will say, 'take ten wickets, take ten wickets.'

A management consultant from KPMG, who happened to be in

India on an assignment, saw Kumble taking all ten. As a boy, he had seen Laker's all ten at Manchester in 1956, his father having taken him to the match. (Similarly Bob Woolmer and, I believe, Mushtaq Mohammed, saw Hanif Mohammed's 499, or its last two hours, and Brian Lara's 501.)

Pakistan won the third Test which was marred by riots. Saeed Anwar carried his bat for 188 out of 316, that's 59.5% of the team's runs. He's in very good company as the following table shows:

Batsman	Venue	Opposition	Runs	Total	%
Graham Gooch	Leeds 1991	West Indies	154	252	61.1%
Saeed Anwar	Calcutta 1999	India	188	316	59.5%
Len Hutton	Oval 1950	West Indies	202	344	58.7%
Len Hutton	Oval 1948	Australia	30	52	57.8%
Len Hutton	Adelaide 50/51	Australia	156	272	56.7%

The list is drawn from memory and is not comprehensive. They're famous instances of batsmen carrying their bat right through an innings (although Hutton was last out at the Oval in 1948).

The World Cup in 1999 was the most exciting, since the inaugural tournament of 1975. I only saw one game live, the Pakistan v. India game in Manchester, which Pakistan lost. Its batting hadn't clicked. Saeed Anwar took time to get going and Inzamam-ul-Haq was in no form at all. But the bowling was so outstanding that Waqar Younis couldn't get in the team. Wasim Akram was partnered by a new star, Shoaib Akhtar. They were followed by high-class young all-rounders, Azhar Mahmood and Abdul Razzaq and there was Saqlain Mushtaq's mesmeric spin, with Mushtaq Ahmed in reserve. I can still recall Shoaib bowling Stephen Fleming and Steve Waugh, both beaten for speed. Also beaten for speed was Sherwin Campbell who went to hook, was late with his stroke and top-edged a six over third man. Saqlain was in top form too but for me the bowler of the tournament was Wasim Akram. Talk about making the ball talk. The delivery that bowled Adam Gilchrist in the first encounter between the two teams was the ball of the tournament.

By the time they got to the final, Saeed Anwar had run into form having scored two centuries. Wasim won the toss and batted as he felt that bowling was the team's strength, chasing wasn't. The batting imploded and Australia, under no pressure, rattled off the runs with half the overs to spare. Shoaib Akhtar was murdered as he kept striving for speed not accuracy. Talk of match fixing resurfaced. Both Mushtaq Mohammed, the manager, and Richard Pybus, the coach, rejected the allegations saying that the players were highly motivated to win. The problem, they said, was that the dressing room had been invaded by the PCB top brass and their families, who behaved as if they'd already won. There was no opportunity for team talk or motivational sessions, no privacy.

We fans saw none of this. All we saw was Saeed Anwar in ominously good form hitting Glenn McGrath for two sumptuous fours and then taking time out to change the rubber grip on the bat handle. Why didn't he do that before he came out? He took ages and succeeded in breaking his own concentration and he was bowled straightaway on resumption. That was just the opening the Aussies needed and Shane Warne and Glenn McGrath did the rest.

Maybe Pakistan blew it, but what Steve Waugh achieved was absolutely astonishing. Having started badly, the only way they could win the Cup was by winning ALL of the remaining seven matches. Unlike Pakistan in 1992, when they needed favourable results in matches they were not involved in, it was all within their control. Nevertheless, it was a stupendous achievement. Sure they had luck. South Africa was beaten because Lance Klusener had a moment of madness and in the final Pakistan imploded, but in both cases it was due to pressure.

I had switched to Sky to watch the World Cup and I have to say that the quality of coverage was superior to the BBC's. This came home to me a couple of years ago when I spent some time converting video recordings to DVD that I had made of BBC highlights. Some deterioration of recording quality is to be expected, but it was clear that BBC used only one camera at each end and there was not the scrutiny of lbws and close-wicket catches and run-outs because the evidence was not there. Much as I admire David Gower, he is an inadequate anchorman as he talks too much and Botham is wasted space, but Atherton and Nasser Hussain are first class and Shane Warne was a revelation last year. BBC's saving graces were Richie Benaud and Jim Laker.

Winning the 1999 World Cup gave Australia the confidence to maintain a remarkable run. Their opponents were usually beaten before they set foot on the field. Indeed, when Pakistan toured Australia immediately after the World Cup, they lost the series 3–0. The second

Test was there for the taking, as they reduced Australia to 126 for five chasing 369. But Adam Gilchrist and Justin Langer, both seeking a regular Test place, put on an double century stand that took them to victory.

The first team to challenge them was India under the combative Saurav Ganguly. The 2001 series was one of the best ever in the history of the game. Having won the first Test, Australia enforced the follow on in the second Test when V. V. S. Laxman and Rahul Dravid put on 376 and then Harbhajan Singh spun the Aussies to defeat. India went on to win the next Test. India is now a major force, not just on the field but also in committee rooms.

England in the meantime were slowly emerging as a force. The slow rebuilding of the English team commenced in 1999 when Duncan Fletcher and Nasser Hussain took over as coach and captain and, crucially, central contracts were introduced. They had to stop losing, identify men with character and develop a nucleus around them which to build a team. Fletcher was an excellent batting coach and spotter of talent, handpicking Marcus Trescothick and Michael Vaughan, neither of whom had an outstanding county record. Freddie Flintoff was selected early, but did not start delivering his early promise for four or five years. Eventually all of the pieces came together by 2004 with a four-man pace attack of Steve Harmison, Matthew Hoggard, Freddie Flintoff and Simon Jones.

We've reached the twenty-first century and I've not yet mentioned the change in the power-base at the heart of cricket. Over-confidence by the West Indians enabled India to win the 1983 World Cup and that unleashed the billion strong television audience of India to cricket viewing. That in turn attracted advertising and sponsorship revenue. Today, some three-quarter of the worldwide revenue to the game accrues through India. The BCCI is more powerful than all the other Boards put together. It has had its downside. Firstly, there's been some score settling by BCCI against the MCC; secondly there is now wall-to-wall cricket including many meaningless one-day matches. However, there are two significant positives. Top players are now extremely well rewarded. Secondly, there is now a new crop of outstanding journalists. Mike

Atherton and Gideon Haigh are worthy successors to John Woodcock and Ray Robinson. Stephen Chalke is a unique new writer shining light on cricketers and matches not covered by others. Simon Wilde, Scyld Berry, Peter Roebuck are going strong.

Kardar wrote a number of cricket books and he wrote well. Other than him, we had to rely on Qamaruddin Butt who, from 1954 to 1967 covered every tour. They were poor books but at least he provided a record. From the text it is clear that on he wasn't actually there on some tours. More recently, Shujauddin Butt and Dr Khadim Hussain Baloch have written some excellent books. India always had good writers and one of these was an active player, Sunil Gavaskar. There are now some outstanding writers from the subcontinent writing for the www. cricinfo. com website. Osman Samiuddin, Dilip Premchandran and Sambit Bal bring objectivity where there used to be sycophancy, felicity of prose where there used to be idiom and error-strewn copy. The outstanding writer from the subcontinent has to be Ramchandra Guha, a sociologist who brings a thoroughness to his research that only David Frith, on a narrower canvas, manages.

Against all these pluses must be set a substantial negative. The game has sold its soul to television. It no longer controls its destiny. Match fixing is a direct consequence of this and is here to stay. Its form might change but betting is widespread.

Betting is illegal in India but is nevertheless widespread. What about Pakistan? More generally why do Islamic countries tolerate betting? Good question. I remember a BBC holiday programme about Dubai. They were interviewing someone in Dubai. The exchange went as follows:

'Isn't gambling illegal in Islam?'

'Yes.'

'Why do you allow betting on horses?'

'We don't'

'You don't? Then what's all this?'

'Oh this is a horse-racing club. You pay a fee to become a member of the club. You are then allowed to forecast the outcome of the race. If you guess correctly, you win a prize. The prize is in proportion to your membership fee.'

Where there's a will there's a way.

16. 2005–2011

In 2004 I was diagnosed as suffering from Parkinson's Disease and on 1ˢᵗ November 2005, I retired. There was no fanfare, no tears; one day I was working, the next I wasn't, as clinical a change of state as death.

It took me quite a while to get used to retirement. It took Kadeeja sometime to get used to me as well. She couldn't figure out how someone who used to be very busy but tidy had now become a slob when he had time to spare. I've always worked best when working against the clock. I'm her complete opposite. Give me a week to do a job that takes a day and I'll put off doing it until the last day. She'd never put off until tomorrow what she could do today. We are chalk and cheese. Together we are fruit salad not smoothie.

Many people thought that I would spend more time watching cricket. I was not so sure. Cricket was, is, an abiding passion, a refuge from the daily grind. If it became a core activity I wasn't sure it would work. Sir James Goldsmith famously said that if you marry your mistress you create a job vacancy. So I had other plans. I can do no better than quote from the e-mail I sent to all my colleagues when I retired.

'

Some of you may be aware that last year I was diagnosed as suffering from Parkinson's Disease. I will never forget the day it was confirmed. Steve, Jackie and I were due to present to the Association of British Insurers our pitch for some research work on Treating Customers Fairly. Although it was Jackie's show, I was in the lead. I was drugged up to my gills with some colouring they had injected into my head the previous evening to get a brain scan. As a result I went to the ABI looking very jaundiced, or as jaundiced as brown skin will permit, and with my mind on the imminent results of the scan. Not surprisingly I fluffed the pitch and I had to apologise to Steve Jackie and Mary without giving any explanation.

Parkinson's arises through the loss of dopamine, a chemical in the brain that control's the coordination of limbs etc. By the time you realise you have a problem you will have lost over 50% of your supply of the chemical. The process can be retarded but not reversed. For the moment, apart from tremors in my right limbs, there have been only two effects. Firstly, my already thin voice has become more so. I have attended a 9-week course in speech therapy. It was very helpful, although I failed in my objective of matching Andrew Smith on decibel count. Secondly, my face has lost some expression. When your own wife says 'Why are you staring at me?' you know you've got a problem. Other people's wives perhaps, but who'd stare at his own wife?

One of the things I want to do early on in retirement is to see if I really can write a novel that has been inside me for the past ten years. At one level it can be described as a block buster set in the insurance industry but at another level it is like a Greek or Wagnerian tragedy with man caught up in the grip of larger forces their background made them ill-equipped to cope with. The plot is OK, writing dialogue is the hard bit. Maybe I should go for the Samuel Beckett approach. The only snag is that I know two people who have indulged such personal fantasies and been unable to get their work published. All logic suggests that I am wasting my time but I've got to give it a try.'

It is common on retirement to look back. The financial services world of the sixties was another world altogether. Not all the changes since then were for the better. In those days the insurance industry had a sense of vocation and social purpose. Management never forgot that they were the custodians of policyholders' money. The directors were paid sensible salaries. There were good perks, subsidised mortgages, good pensions but they were all designed to engender loyalty. Customers' interests were always put first; admittedly, it was the company who decided what those interests were, they didn't ask the customers. The problem is that insurance is about pooling of risks, the healthy subsidising the infirm, saving from the fat years supporting the lean years, investment-wise. The modern society with it's ****-you-Jack-I'm alright, is inimical to it.

Social cohesiveness has gone. It is strange that whilst technology and air travel has brought people physically closer we seem to be drifting further apart. Even a tiny country like Britain is now devolving autonomy to Scotland, Wales etc. In the City, the biggest change is that limited liability companies are now run for the benefit of the executive directors who expropriate an unreasonable slice of the cake. A major success has been the growth of personal finance journalism. Many of them, mainly ladies have done an excellent job. Unfortunately there are a few who, if they had one more brain cell, they'd be amoebas.

Once I'd got my bearings, I joined a Creative Writing Class and this book is one of the results; there are two others. The first book, *The Herd Instinct of Mules*, was set in a bank that was taking outrageous risks and nearly went bust when an external calamity struck. Unfortunately, the credit crunch took place whilst the book was in its final stages. Suddenly life was imitating and exaggerating art. I was showing losses in millions whereas the real banks were losing billions. The novel was completed but is lying in my drawer. Most people are innumerate and if it was only the size of the losses, I might have fought on. But I was still learning the craft of writing. Writing a novel is not the same as writing a report. I had to do some unlearning.

The next novel, *Educating Majid,* is ready. It's a rites-of-passage story of a bright but naive actuary. It deals mainly with insurance frauds and boardroom skullduggery. Soon I'll be burning electronic shoe leather in search of an agent, no publisher being willing to take on a new writer of fiction if they don't have one. The novel after that, a celestial Dirty Dozen or Mean Machine, is being fleshed out.

In May 2005 we had arranged a dinner with a client of Ian Clark whom we had assisted in buying a life insurance company. The venue was The Smiths in Farringdon. However the day coincided with the UEFA Cup Final between Liverpool and AC Milan. We could not change the date of the final as we had no say in the matter. Nor could we change the date of the dinner as we had no say in the matter of the client's diary. So we decided to bring the dinner forward to 6pm. If we ate quickly, we could spend the rest of the evening in the bar downstairs watching the match on television. The client was late and Liverpool were one nil down before we sat down. Then Ian Clark kept getting text messages, Liverpool 2–0 and then 3–0 down. With the match as good as lost, we switched the mobile off and had a leisurely dinner. When we went downstairs and walked past the bar, incredibly the match was still on; Liverpool had overcome three-goal deficit, been through the extra time and had just won the penalty shoot out. And we'd missed it all.

Pakistan cricket staggered along firstly under Moin Khan then Waqar Younis and finally Inzamam-ul-Haq. It could still produce amazing cricket but also snatch defeat from the jaws of victory. A classic example was a game against the West Indies in 1999 when Wasim Akram bowled his team towards a magnificent win. Courtney Walsh, who holds the world record for the most Test ducks, joined Jimmy Adams for the last wicket only for Saqlain Mushtaq to so lose his head that he made a hash of two easy run-outs. It was so crass that thoughts of match-fixing haunted me.

I last saw a Pakistan game, other than on television, in the 20:20 World Cup match at Lord's when Pakistan beat South Africa. Again the Pakistan supporters had boorish elements. India had just been knocked out and one guy was wearing a T-shirt with the legend 'I bought my ticket off an Indian Supporter'. Another group of supporters were walking around the ground chanting 'You'll never win the Ashes'. Gratuitous incitement more appropriate to a football ground than a cricket one.

I couldn't have wished for a better end to my working life than the Ashes series of 2005. In terms of the ebb and flow of fortunes and the closeness of many of the games it rivalled the 1960/61 Worrell/Benaud series. This time we could see it live on television. We could see history being made. I can still remember the final day of the Edgbaston Test. My brother and his family, who live in Toronto, were coming to visit us and I had to pick them up from Epsom railway station. I went early but couldn't find any parking space. So I drove to the Sainsbury superstore and waited in the car park until the match was over. Who cares if my brother had to wait? I sat listening intently to the commentary, unaware that practically every car in the row had a bloke doing the same thing. When Geraint Jones eventually caught Mike Kasprowicz down the leg side you should have heard the roar that emerged from the cars.

The next Test was just as exciting. Aren't Warne and Lee fierce competitors? Having been able to set England only a modest target, they tore through the top order. Then Flintoff steadied the ship until, with victory but a dozen runs away, Lee bowled Fred with a screaming delivery. I hid behind the sofa not daring to watch Matthew Hoggard and Ashley Giles implode. But they didn't. Hoggard, James Anderson's role model as a stroke-less blocker, unfolded an exquisite cover drive and the tension was lifted.

Even then, the Ashes weren't in the bag. Australia could draw the series and retain it if they won at the Oval. It all hinged on the final day. What cruel irony that the man who did most to keep Australia in with a chance during the series dropped a simple catch that reprieved Pietersen.

Deloitte's offices are a stone's throw from Fleet Street. The entire office, apart from the senior partner, who's more used to receiving than giving adulation, were on the pavement as the victory parade made its way, at dirge-like speed down the street. The sight of Flintoff eyes glazed over should have been a warning of things to come but on that day we begrudged the talisman nothing.

That series was the most exciting Ashes series since 1936/7 or even 1902. Alas it represented the summit of our achievement rather than a stage on a longer journey. Injuries were the problem; first Michael Vaughan and Simon Jones then Freddie Flintoff then Marcus Trescothick, depriving the team of four of its key players. Of these, Trescothick was the biggest loss, particularly in the one-day team.

The Australians exacted a terrible revenge in the return series in 2006/7. Flintoff was inadequate as captain and the series was lost 5–0. And yet things could have been so different. Having lost the first Test, in the second at Adelaide, England rattled up over 550 and then declared. A couple of wickets were taken and then a crucial catch was dropped. Ricky Ponting was missed by Ashley Giles. Even then the Australian first innings ended after tea on the fourth day, giving England a lead of thirty-eight runs and the match was petering out to a draw on a flat slow pitch. Then, on the final day, Warne mesmerised them not through exceptional bowling, but sheer force of personality. It was the most sickening defeat I've come across. The saddest part was that I actually woke up at two in the morning to watch it. I'm struggling to find an appropriate analogy for the capitulation. Perhaps lambs to the slaughter best describes their meek submission.

It took England a couple of years and a few stumbles before they found the right formula, Andy Strauss as captain and Andy Flower as coach, both sharing a common vision and were at one on how to achieve it. As they implemented their formula they were lucky that Australia were on their way down. We regained the Ashes in England in 2009, not by playing the better cricket throughout but by winning the sessions that mattered. Then last winter Australia were completely stuffed. The cricket was exciting to watch because the hitherto unbeatable was being overwhelmed. Every time we were down (Perth apart) someone would instigate a comprehensive fight-back. England had become the new Australia. Anderson was a revelation in Adelaide and Perth; Trott is a major find, an English player who simply loves batting; and Strauss is a superb captain; a tad defensive but otherwise the complete package.

It was therefore disappointing to see the subsequent performance in the World Cup. The fighting spirit led to several close matches but the skill levels were not sufficient. It was strange to hear Graeme Swann say that England were the new Pakistan, referring to 1992; you can't ape a fluke. The truth is that the World Cup was not as important as the Ashes series to either the ECB or the players. India the eventual winners had been planning for 18 months carefully rotating players to keep them fit and ready.

Two changes on the domestic front is a neat way to introduce some pleasant news before I round off this personal journey on a more serious note.

Deena decided to change career and become a lawyer. I was a proud father when I went to the Law Society's offices to watch her collect her diploma. Two years on she is now a fully fledged solicitor. Like her mother she has a tidy logical mind and is tailor-made for the legal profession.

Zamin, after getting his PhD worked in computers for a few years and then became a member of the genome project where he is bringing his knowledge of computers and statistical analysis to complement the geneticists. Recently he married Susie Ross, whose father is, would you believe it, an actuary?

17. Opium of the Asses

In the final chapter I trace the origin of Pakistan but, whatever its antecedents, it has certainly become an aggressively Muslim country.

The antagonism to Hindus seems pathological. I cannot speak for the people at large, but it is something that has poisoned the minds of cricketers. Kardar, in his first book, *Inaugural Test Matches,* talks of having chided Maulana Abul Kalam Azad, a noted scholar and minister in the Indian Government, for opting to stay in a 'Hindu country'. Fazal Mahmood in his autobiography refers to Hindus as if it were a stigma. More recently, when Ehsan Mani was made President of the ICC, Sarfaraz Nawaz asked how he could represent Pakistan when he was a Hindu (which Mani denied being).

Having said that, the selectors have generally looked at the skill levels rather than creed. So far six (possibly seven) non-Muslims have represented Pakistan: four Christians: Wallis Mathias, Duncan Sharpe, Antao D'Souza, and Yousuf Youhana; and two Hindus: the cousins Anil Dalpat and Danish Keneria. It has been suggested that Khalid Ibadulla is Christian but I have no corroboration of it. In addition, a Parsi, Rusi Dinshaw, toured India in 1952/3 but did not play in a Test. Wallis Mathias and Danish Keneria both had extended runs in the Test team, Mathias as the country's first good slip fieldsman and a reliable lower middle order batsmen. His career only ended after the disastrous 1962 tour. The same tour ended Antao D'Souza's career. Yusuf Youhana was so patently a class act that Wasim Akram made him one of his first picks in the batting line-up. Interestingly, criticism of him really only surfaced after he'd converted to Islam. Younis Khan, in one of his brief spells as captain threatened to drop him because of his poor fielding. Quite right too.

Danish, a bowler of great skill but limited guile, has been an integral part of the bowling unit for some years and may continue to be, if he can resolve the outstanding issues re 'match-fixing'. Anil Dalpat might have had an extended run, had Imran not preferred the combativeness of Salim Yousuf.

That just leaves Duncan Sharpe. He was perhaps unlucky not to be picked for the Indian tour of 1960/61. He played in all three Tests against Australia in 1958/9 and performed adequately, no more, averaging twenty-two with a top score of fifty-six. He emigrated to South Australia for, it would appear, economic reasons, rather than to further his cricketing career. Ian Chappell, then new to Test cricket, was surprised to learn that the unassuming groundsman at Adelaide had played for Pakistan against Australia.

So I have no concerns about bias against non-Muslims in the selection process. Offhand, I cannot think of a player who should have been selected but wasn't on account of his faith. My concern is about the gradual Islamisation of the Test team in this century. The problem arose when Inzamam became captain. His tenure as captain was a particularly sterile one. In much the same way as Viv Richards had made his team a symbol of Afro-supremacy, Inzamam tried to make his team an Islamic beacon. Team prayers were introduced. Coach Bob Woolmer couldn't fit in tactical and motivational talks. Anyway, how does that encourage team spirit when Yusuf Youhana and Danish Kaneria aren't Muslims?

A man's religion is a personal matter. Prayers, incantations and rituals represent his personal communion with God. They're less important than honesty, probity and loyalty to one's brethren (the team). Today every television interview begins with the statement, 'First of all, praise be to Allah,' or its Arabic equivalent. Why is it necessary to say that? To prove that you're a good Muslim? If so, prove it to whom? Yourself, or to others or to God? Whichever of the three it is, it is deeds that matter not words.

Anyway, the evidence is not compelling. Many of the players with ostentatious show of Islamic fervour (Inzamam included) are those who did not get a clean bill of health from Qayyum, whereas some others who do not flaunt their religion, such as Shoaib and Younis Khan, have not provoked the ire of Qayyum. One day we will find out why Yousuf Youhana became a Muslim. Much been made of his rich vein of form since then. So what, there may be many reasons for that.

Another by-product of this Islamisation that Bob Woolmer referred

158

to was a fatalism induced by the belief that 'whatever God wills, will happen'. If you believe that God is omniscient and knows everything then it is tautological to say that he knows the outcome before it happens. But that is not the same as saying *Que sera sera,* whatever will be, will be. I always remember my father saying, 'God helps those who help themselves' and Thomas Carlyle saying (OK I read about it, he was long since gone before I arrived) that 'Genius is 99% perspiration and 1% inspiration.'

To the narrow-minded clerics who've taken such a hold on the players, I'll misquote C. L. R. James and say, 'What do they know of Islam who only Islam know?'

Listen to contrary views, be open to criticism and learn from others. That was what Prophet Muhammad did.

18. My Dream Team

This chapter is pure self indulgence. I have selected eleven players who've given me most pleasure and whom I see most often in my dreams. They do not form a well-balanced team, but what the heck! Don Bradman selected his team full of poor fielders and a batsman light. My team is as follows.

1. Saeed Anwar
2. Majid Khan
3. David Gower
4. Rahul Dravid
5. Peter May
6. Garry Sobers
7. Imtiaz Ahmed (w-k)
8. Imran Khan
9. Wasim Akram
10. Shane Warne (captain)
11. Jimmy Anderson

Reserves: Ian Botham, Ted Dexter, Tom Graveney, Marcus Trescothick, Mark Waugh, Sachin Tendulkar, Alan Knott, Graeme Swann, Bishen Bedi and Waqar Younis.

Four batsmen who won't give it away (Dravid, May, Sobers and Imran) to balance four who would keep you on the edge of your seats (Saeed, Majid, Gower and Imtiaz). I urge readers to get out DVDs (or YouTube) of Saeed Anwar and Majid Khan's batting. I wish there was adequate footage of Peter May. A forgotten man now, he was regarded by many as the best English batsman post WW2. Note that none of Lloyds' bullies is selected.

Saeed Anwar is a poor fielder; Imran only adequate. Wasim and May are better but not special; the others are excellent fielders, Sobers, Gower and Anderson being exceptional. For the slips, the choice is from Majid, Dravid, Sobers, Warne and Anderson. Cover point is Gower; May is gully, Sobers can go anywhere especially short leg. Majid and Anderson are excellent outfielders.

The bowling attack is unbalanced; three swing bowlers, two of whom are left-handers. Really, I should drop Jimmy and play Swann or Bedi, possibly Swann as Bedi is an average fielder. But right now I cannot contemplate life without Jimmy.

Saeed Anwar was one of the best one-day players and played one of the greatest one-day innings ever (194 against India). He built up an exceptional Test record too. A beautiful timer of the ball, strong wrists enabled him to play many shots square of the wicket. A hopeless fielder, a family tragedy curtailed his career.

Majid played cricket as one imagined was played in the golden age. Always walked when he knew he was out. Another beautiful timer of the ball and a thrilling player of fast bowling. Between '72 and '77 he was one of the top cricketers in the world.

Cardus has written eloquently about Frank Woolley and every time I read it, I am reminded of David Gower. His timing was exceptional and his placement precise.

*Utterly self-effacing, to me Rahul Dravid is greater than Sachin Tendulkar.
As we saw in England in 2011, he gets going when the going gets tough.
Ostensibly defensive, nevertheless he scores a high proportion of
his runs in boundaries.*

*Peter Barker Howard May, the world's best batsman by some distance, in
the mid-fifties. An amateur with a professional's hunger.
Had the best on-drive in the business.*

166

Don Bradman said Garry Sobers was the greatest cricketer ever. 'What, greater than you?' asked his biographer. 'Yes, I was only a batsman.' For an attacking batsman he had a water-tight defence, as a left-arm swing bowler he was in the Akram/Davidson class; as an all-purpose fielder he was beyond compare.

Imtiaz Ahmed, had a fearless approach to fast bowling. In pre-helmet days he used to give Tyson, Gilchrist and Hall the charge. Safe, unobtrusive wicket keeper.

By dint of self-improvement, Imran Khan became the best of his era, second only to Sobers in my time, although there is a big gap between the two. An orthodox batsman and, at his two-year peak, the most complete fast bowler of his time.

Wasim Akram could make the ball talk. He was too good for his own good, often beating the bat and confounding the umpires. Watch on YouTube his delivery to Robert Croft whose path was too sinuous for the umpire to detect a plumb lbw.

*Mike Atherton reckoned Shane Warne was the cleverest bowler in out-
thinking a batsman. The greatest spin bowler of my time, shading Bishen
Bedi, a fine slip and a useful batsman. He stole the 2006/7 Adelaide
Test from England in broad daylight. Should make an interesting and
imaginative captain.*

James Anderson is the most complete fast bowler currently playing; and one of the best fielders in the world. very athletic with prehensile hands.

19. Shattered Dreams

It is time we faced up to some truths. Pakistan cricket has regularly failed the smell test. Suspicion of foul play has appeared all too often, for all of them to be untrue. As the journey of this book reaches its end, the conclusion is that there is systemic failure in how the country and its cricket are run.

Pakistan is a young nation, having been created, by accident, in August 1947. Its founder Jinnah, a non-practising Muslim, was an ardent believer in a United India. It was only when Nehru opposed proportional representation that Jinnah changed course and insisted on a separate country for the Muslims of India. He got his way because the Attlee Government wanted to get rid of India to concentrate on the problems facing post-war UK. Of course, Pakistan was not the only option open to the Muslims of India: they could opt to remain in secular India. Today there are actually more Muslims in India than in Pakistan. Although there have been clashes, notably in Gujarat, they live in comparative freedom and prosperity as part of one of the emerging major nations. Pakistan meanwhile is a political and economic basket-case.

This contrast is particularly galling to Pakistanis. It is as if, in 1947, Muslims were given two sealed envelopes to choose from and those who opted for Pakistan chose the wrong one. For Pakistani cricketers, who have an unshakeable belief, not without merit until now, that theirs is the better cricket team, the inability to participate in the riches of the Indian Premier League is acutely disappointing.

Had the British Government and Nehru the slightest inkling that Jinnah was terminally ill, they'd have postponed the transfer of power by a year and thereby avoided the partitioning of India. Think what a cricket team we'd have had with bowlers from Pakistan and batsmen from India!

Jinnah envisaged a secular not a theocratic state, but he died early in 1948 before he had fully thought through the details of the constitution. His deputy was assassinated. Pakistan therefore had no guiding purpose, no role models, no constitution and no direction. Crucially, it had no history. It is impossible to describe its history without describing the history of the subcontinent. All power would be seen to have been held in Delhi, making Pakistan appear to be a satellite country.

This was a serious problem for educationists. The result was to deify Jinnah and ascribe to him qualities that he did not possess. A brilliant lawyer of great probity, he was a cold fish; a man to be admired not loved; not a man of the people and, above all, not really a Muslim. Another result was to demonise India and Hindus. Young men grew up with a distorted view of Hindus, in much the same way as Israeli Jews are growing up hating Arabs and young Palestinians, Jews.

Adding further to the identity confusion, the newly minted national anthem was written in Persian which is like *God Save the Queen* or *Land of Hope and Glory* being written in Latin. We used to recite it regularly but it was only marginally more penetrable than the Qu'ran. The only phrase I understood was, *'parcham-e- sitara-o-hilal'*, which in Urdu means 'the standard of star and crescent' and presumably meant the same in Persian.

A series of opportunists ran the country before the army took over in 1958. After a brief period of pseudo-democracy in the seventies, the army took over again. In the years that followed, pseudo-democrats and the army were to play pass the parcel. Each outgoing or ousted leader was accused of corruption on a grand scale by their successor. People did not know but suspected it to be true ('perks of office').

In the past thirty years, the country has reinvented itself as an Islamic state but there is no justification for it. It is not where the religion originated, which is Saudi Arabia; nor is it the country with the most Muslims, which is Indonesia.

Today cricket is the only thing that unites the nation. The politicians are corrupt, the society is feudal, the political system is dysfunctional, there is a sharp divide between the urban educated and the rest, between Punjab and Sindh on the one hand and the tribal frontierland. The latter are Pushto-speaking people who are of Afghan stock. Talibans, who were thrown out of Afghanistan by the Russians in the eighties now control large regions of Pakistan and are resented by the locals.

Islamic fundamentalism has found many adherents. This is exported out of Saudi Arabia who finance a lot of madrassahs that teach Wahhabi interpretation of Islam. But they couldn't have succeeded if the audience was not receptive. With none of the political and legal institutions inspiring trust, people found it reassuring to relate to a brand of religion that relied on literal interpretation of guidelines enunciated 1400 years ago.

That then is the socio-political background. Pakistan played its first international, against West Indies, in 1948. In 1952 they beat a visiting MCC team. On the strength of that, they got Test status later that year and a tour of England in 1954. Kardar led that side. Unexpectedly they beat England at the Oval. Suddenly Pakistan was good at something. All the players, especially Hafeez Kardar, Fazal Mahmood and Hanif Mohammed, became national heroes. In the next few years they beat full-strength Australia and the West Indies. A fallow period followed before a second coming in the seventies which lasted thirty years.

Most of the early cricketers were drawn from universities. Of the team that beat England at the Oval in 1954, eight were graduates, whereas England had only Peter May (Frank Tyson obtained his degree later). They were cultured to the point of deference. Wisden said, 'The players were splendid ambassadors. Rarely has a more popular set of cricketers toured anywhere.' In the sixties they acquired the tag of being good losers. That changed after exposure to Ian Chappell and Packer Cricket. Mushtaq Mohammed introduced combativeness and Imran Khan mental toughness.

In sixty years there have been only two captains, Hafeez Kardar and Imran Khan who have managed to instil a common purpose and unity in the team. Both were autocratic, not one of the lads. Both had the last say in team selection and were unafraid to back their own judgment. Kardar had the halo of an Oxford education, which mattered at the time; Imran was unquestionably the best player in the team, a match-winner. Their successors had to deal with team dissent. It's not that they did not have problems themselves. Kardar and Khan Mohammad didn't get on; but Kardar had other bowlers to fall back on. Imran Khan and Javed Miandad were chalk and cheese but both put team interests first.

During the eighties Pakistan were the only team that gave the mighty West Indies a serious contest, not losing a series to them from 1982 onwards. From 1985–1988 they were the second-best team in the world.

People marvel at Pakistan's capacity to churn out talented cricketers in spite of all the problems. They are right to marvel. Schools and universities used to be the breeding ground. Not any more, the facilities are no longer there. At the same time winning the World Cup in 1992 has increased television coverage and top cricketers have become superstars. Kids in villages and towns started emulating them. This has thrown up remarkable natural talents, people such as Yusuf Youhana, Younis Khan, Shahid Afridi. Mohammed Amir, Inzamam-ul-Haq and a host of others. They are unpolished diamonds, inarticulate and lacking in education and sophistication. They make embarrassing ambassadors when speaking to the media. We can't blame the players for the circumstances in which they grew up. We can blame the PCB have failed in their duty to arrange coaching in social skills,

I had regarded cricket as a metaphor for all that is good and desirable in life: justice, fair play, sportsmanship and what Neville Cardus called the typical British compromise between individual goals and corporate responsibility. Sure Pakistani cricketers often fell short of it but I was sure that these were failures in execution rather than intent. Thus umpires might make honest mistakes but will not deliberately cheat. The same went for players and I had role models in Imtiaz Ahmed and Majid Khan. As I noted in an earlier chapter, I regretted that greater combativeness led some of the players of the last twenty years to compromise their integrity and cheat.

However in the last decade I was in for a rude shock. A spate of biographies and autobiographies of the stars of the 1950s came out. Perhaps it was an urge to tell the truth, to put the record straight; or perhaps it was a cathartic confession as they prepared to meet their Maker. Either way some of my childhood idols appeared to have feet of clay. Let me give a few examples.

Rajinder Amarnath wrote a biography of his father Lala Amarnath based upon extended tape recorded interviews. Lala managed the Indian team that toured Pakistan under Vinoo Mankad in 1954/55. Immediately before the fifth Test in Karachi, Hafeez Kardar, invited Lala to tea.

I entered the room and occupied the sofa with my back to the door. After a while someone knocked on the door and wished Kardar. He

then said, 'Any instructions for tomorrow's game skipper?' I turned my head to see who it was. The man was none other than Idris Baig, one of the umpires named for the Test. 'What instructions do you want?' I said. Seeing me Baig rushed out but the great plan to defeat India had been revealed. I looked at Kardar who was visibly shaken.

Lala was a wonderful raconteur and we cannot rule out the possibility that he might have, if not fabricated, at least embellished the story. The same cannot be said of Shujauddin, a regular member of the Pakistan team during 1954/56 and a cultured and reliable witness. He wrote a book on Pakistan cricket Babes of Cricket to World Champion. In it he makes no reference to this incident, not surprising as he wasn't there, but he did say that, at Lala's request, Idris Beg was replaced as the umpire for that Test. When writing about Donald Carr's MCC 'A' team that toured in 1955, Shuja said:

… it was during the course of this match that a number of umpiring decisions were given some of which were questioned justifiably by the visitors … Granted that there were a couple of rank bad lbw decisions against the tourists given by Idris Beg …

I interviewed Shuja in 1997 and he was more candid face-to-face than in print. Idris Beg was in love with himself and believed that people came to see him umpire rather than to watch the game. He took orders from Kardar. In the Peshawar 'Test' against MCC 'A', four of Kardar's eleven-wicket haul were lbw. Shuja said that none of them was out. Kardar was bowling left arm round the wicket, the ball was hardly turning and the batsmen were well forward. Idris Beg was the umpire in every case.

In his *At the Heart of English Cricket,* Stephen Chalke's biography of Geoffrey Howard, the diligent and affable manager of Donald Carr's team, there is a reference to a meeting called by Pakistan's President, Iskandar Mirza, immediately after the end of the acrimonious series.

(Mirza) summoned Geoffrey Howard and Hafeez Kardar to talks and he listened carefully to what the two had to say. From the England perspective there had been a catalogue of bad umpiring decisions in each of the representative matches, almost all of them at their expense.

… From the Pakistan side the umpires had done their best and the tourists had shown insufficient respect both in querying decisions and in subjecting Idris Begh to a soaking.…

Iskander Mirza paused before drawing his conclusion …

'Having listened to what you had to say, Mr Howard, and to you Abdul Hafeez, I have to say that I form the view that Idris Begh, as an umpire, is a cheat.'

'But he's the best we've got,' Hafeez protested.

'The best umpire? Or the best cheat?'

So Kardar was cut from the same cloth as Miandad. OK, he was educated and more of a boardroom bruiser than a street-fighter but that was just a veneer. More shattering were allegations that Imtiaz was not quite the paragon I had imagined him to be. Roland Perry in his biography of Keith Miller accused him of standing his ground when, early in his groundbreaking 138 against the Australian Services XI, a thick edge had been caught by second slip; worse, in Stephen Chalke's book, Howard accuses Imtiaz of claiming a catch when he'd caught it on the half-volley.

Hanif Mohammed in his autobiography referred to his days as a schoolboy who was coached by Abdul Aziz, former All India wicket-keeper (and the father of Salim Durrani). Abdul Aziz often umpired and it was not unknown for Hanif to be given a second life by Aziz failing to raise his finger even when he was patently out. His argument was that Hanif needed time in the middle to improve his batting. As he was so obviously a rising star, such bending of the rules was in the national interest. It is not improbable that such generosity extended to first-class matches.

Next, consider ball tampering: a very difficult crime to prove. There is no doubt that there is skill in bowling reverse swing and that a number of Pakistan bowlers are adept at it. Most people regard Sarfraz Nawaz as the pioneer although Mushtaq Mohammed refers to Geoff Arnold bowling it in Pakistan in 1972/73. Imtiaz Ahmed says that Khan Mohammad practiced it in the fifties. Now of course several bowlers from other countries have mastered it and it contributed in no small measure to England's Ashes win in 2005 and 2010/11. It is also true that scuffing one side of the ball by illegal means accelerates the process and accentuates the effect. As spotting it is particularly difficult, it must happen more frequently than on the few occasions they've been identified.

What of match-fixing? To their credit, when it first surfaced in the mid-nineties, the Pakistan Cricket Board set up the Qayyum enquiry, a detailed piece of work. The opportunity was there to clean up the game with exemplary punishments. Majid Khan, then the Chief Executive of the Pakistan Cricket Board was determined to do so. Instead he was replaced. Several key players did not turn up and suffered only minor fines for 'non-attendance'.

At around the same time the cricket team became Islamised. It started with Saeed Anwar after a personal tragedy but the transformation was completed under the captaincy of Inzamam. Younis Youhana, hitherto defiantly Christian, converted to Islam.

Readers can form their own views. All I would say is that many Pakistanis in other walks of life have made a Faustian pact with Satan or, as Muslims call him, Shaitan. This enables them to engage in bribery, tax evasion and general fiscal impropriety but retaining the trappings of a devout Muslim. If politicians, financiers and businessmen are comfortable with such an approach, why is it a surprise if someone else whose day job is playing sport, does the same? The only Commandment that matters is the eleventh: 'Thou shall not be found out'.

If only the Congress Party and Nehru had listened to Jinnah and given Muslims proportional representation, this problem would have been averted. We can't put the clock back. No Pakistani politician could contemplate reintegration back into India. There are far too many hotheads ready to take their life. In any case India has its own challenges keeping the current union intact. In life you have to deal with the cards you've been dealt.

It is difficult to see how things can get better without a sharp shock to the system. People are all too ready to blame others rather than look inwardly at their own conduct. Nor is there an administrative body which is strong, independent and far-sighted. It pains me when cricketers or the administrators claim victory when in reality it is simply that they have not been caught. There have been several matches that defy comprehension, the most recent being the Sydney Test of 2010. Last summer my excitement was immense upon seeing Mohammad Amir in action. His repertoire and control at such a tender age was astonishing. I genuinely thought that I was seeing the greatest since Sidney Barnes.

And then came the match-fixing scandal. Michael Holding wasn't the only one reduced to tears at the cynical corruption of such precocious talent.

I remember being told as a child that hell is a furnace in which your body burns, is then made whole and burns again, in a continuous process until kingdom gone. I don't believe in heaven and hell but that is the type of punishment that is appropriate for the people (from the betting industry and from the team) who corrupted Amir.

This is not the team I was drawn to in 1954/55. But in a hark back to my childhood all those years ago, the Chairman of PCB, the man who had made some ill-considered remarks about the English cricket team when the spot-fixing scandal emerged last year was Ijaz Butt, the very same who'd been awarded school colours by St Mary's.

The criminal investigation of Salman Butt, Mohammed Asif and Mohammed Amir has barely got going and may drag on. Meanwhile the ICC announced its verdict. Net of suspended sentence each of them is out of the game for five years. Exemplary and necessary but is it sufficient to clean up the game? How many players have not been caught? Salim Malik, Azharuddin, Hansie Cronje and Salman Butt, clearly captains are targeted by the fixers. Were there other captains who've escaped detection?

Why is Younis Khan unable to hold on to the job of captain? Is he the one clean player? I am afraid the issue has not gone away. If there are still players in the thrall of the fixers, how would they break free?

I find it repugnant that the recent ODI and T20 captain is a cheat, not just a cheat but a stupid cheat. Shahid Afridi has twice been caught on camera, once damaging the pitch at good length level with his spikes and once biting off bits of ball leather.

The big problem in implementing change is the absence of probity in the administrative body. Over the years there have been three or four unimpeachable characters but the recent ones have been eased out. No one has any faith in the selection process and there is suspicion of their motives. I remember reading an article about David Murray the West Indies cricketer who paid the price for taking part in a rebel tour of South Africa. His subsequent ostracisation made him descend into drug-dependancy. He said, 'It's all very well for the administrators with their two cars, two houses and wives and mistresses, to ask us cricketers not to tour South Africa. We've no income outside of tours if we don't get a county contract. How do they expect us to live?' *(The words are mine)*. No doubt many Pakistani cricketers feel the same.

The moral values of a nation may be no business of a sporting body but when it begins to infect the fabric of the sport they have a duty to intervene. Banning South Africa played an important part in its transformation; the more recent banning of Zimbabwe has helped sort out the cricketing organisation.

ICC should ban Pakistan until further notice. Pakistan must then start putting their administrative house in order. They should then offer 'amnesty' to all current players involved in fixing ('truth and reconciliation'). Past players investigated by Qayyum should be followed up and the letter of Qayyum's recommendations implemented. Then, after a three-year period (any longer would kill the game), re-entry can be contemplated. OK, a lot of promising careers would be blighted. Think of the Pollock brothers, Barry Richards, Mike Proctor, Peter Kirsten, Clive Rice – indeed, a whole generation of South Africans. What Pakistan needs is an Ali Bacher at a cricketing level and a Nelson Mandela at the political level. Is that likely?

I am deeply pessimistic. The least I can do is to renounce them. Writing this book has been cathartic. As I write these lines, the England has become the number one team in the world, the position they occupied when I first started my love affair with the game. I no longer have split loyalties. I'm marrying my mistress. I'm supporting England.

Let me end on a positive note. England are playing superlative cricket, have a strong team ethos and unbelievable bench strength in the fast bowling department. Best English team ever? I can only go back to the end of WW2. Set out in the table overleaf are six possible contenders. They're all actual teams. Have a look at them. What do you think?

Oval 1953	Oval 1957	Sydney 1970/1	Leeds 1981	Leeds 2005	Lords 2011
Hutton	Richardson	Boycott	Gooch	Treskothick	Strauss
Edrich	Sheppard	Luckhurst	Boycott	Strauss	Cook
May	Graveney	Edrich	Brearley	Vaughan	Trott
Graveney	May	Fletcher	Gower	Bell	Pietersen
Compton	Cowdrey	D'Oliviera	Gatting	Pietersen	Bell
Bailey	Bailey	Illingworth	Willey	Flintoff	Morgan
Evans	Evans	Knott	Botham	Jones, G	Prior
Laker	Lock	Snow	Taylor	Giles	Broad
Lock	Trueman	Lever	Dilley	Hoggard	Swann
Bedser	Laker	Underwood	Old	Harmison	Tremlett
Trueman	Loader	Willis	Willis	Jones, S	Anderson

Bench strength

Oval 1953	Oval 1957	Sydney 1970/1	Leeds 1981	Leeds 2005	Lords 2011
Statham	Statham	Shuttleworth	Hendrick	Tremlett	Bresnan
Wardle	Tyson	Wilson	Embury	Anderson	Onions
Tattersall	Wardle	Cowdrey	Edmonds	Collingwood	Finn
Simpson	Tattersall	Hampshire	Allott		Rashid
Watson			Tavare		Bopara
Sheppard					Taylor

Only Hutton and Bedser (1953), May (1957), Knott and Snow (1970/1) and Botham (1981) displayed form in the series that merited a place amongst the all-time greats. How many would have merited a place in a World XI in that year? Obviously this is subjective but my World XI squad for each of these years would include only the following:

Oval 1953	Oval 1957	Sydney 1970/1	Leeds 1981	Leeds 2005	Lords 2011
Hutton	May	Boycott	Botham	Trescothick	Cook
Evans	Evans	Knott	Taylor	Pieterson	Trott
Laker	Lock	Snow		Flintoff	Bell
Bedser	Laker				Swann
	Trueman				Anderson

Clearly the quality of cricketers in non-English teams (e.g. in 1981) has a bearing here.

Let us now consider how many had top-class fielders:

Oval 1953	Oval 1957	Sydney 1970/1	Leeds 1981	Leeds 2005	Lords 2011
Lock	Lock		Gower	Trescothick	Trott
Trueman	Trueman		Botham	Flintoff	Bell
					Swann
					Anderson

And now, for the litmus test, how many were average to poor fielders:

Oval 1953	Oval 1957	Sydney 1970/1	Leeds 1981	Leeds 2005	Lords 2011
Laker	Sheppard	Edrich	Boycott	Giles	Cook
Compton	Laker	Luckhurst	Willis	Hoggard	Tremlett
Edrich	Loader	Fletcher		Harmison	
		D'Oliviera			
		Illingworth			
		Lever			
		Underwood			
		Snow			

It is often suggested that we have fewer great players. The mind has a tendency to concertina the past and assume that all the great players were contemporaneous and forget the mediocre ones. Two facts we can say categorically is that the overall standard of fielding is much better today and that New Zealand, India and Pakistan are no longer whipping boys; but there again, what about Bangladesh and West Indies?

The 1953 team faced Australia who had Lindwall in peak form, but with no support. Miller was off-form, Bill Johnston was injured and the rest were rookie bowlers. Then they faced West Indies who had a strong batting line up but thin bowling. The 1957 side having just surrendered a 2–0 lead to South Africa played West Indies with a mixture of ageing and not yet ready players. England in 1981 faced Australia riven by dissent with only Marsh, Lillee and Alderman worth mentioning. The 2005 side certainly faced a great Australian side, but one on its way down. It was going further down when the 2011 side met them.

Whilst the evidence on the quality of opposition is inconclusive, the earlier analysis of England's strengths suggests that only the 1953 team would come near the current team in terms of quality of the team and its bench strength. If we measure the players on their form at the time rather than at their best, I think the current team would score. Edrich and Compton were past their best and May and Graveney hadn't reached theirs, nor had Trueman; whereas with the present team, if Cook, Trott, Bell and Anderson are not at their best, the mind boggles at how good they may become; only Strauss is underperforming. Flower is an outstanding manager, single-minded, fair but ruthless and, as his own career demonstrated, a firm believer in continuous self-improvement. If he can find a way of making those on the fringes remain motivated, then we may well have a dynasty fit to replace Australia and West Indies.

The irony of the Gooch work ethic being the basis of the team's success is not lost on me. Another irony is how poor Illingworth's side comes out. Predictably, Ray himself, when asked how the present team compared with his, said, misquoting Dr W. G. Grace, 'Give me Jimmy.'

I hope the journey has been as rewarding for you as it has been therapeutic for me. I have laid myself bare, not so much warts and all, more warts and warts. I thought I could write with candour about my intellectual inconsistencies as a gap of forty years gives a sense of detachment. But alas I'm no different today. My animosity towards the *News of The World* after their callous destruction of Mohammed Amir turned to hatred of News Corporation when the phone-hacking scandal emerged. A couple of months ago I resolved to hit Murdoch where it hurt most. I decided to cancel my *Times* online subscription and my Sky TV subscription.

Did I do it?

No Sir. 'I will do it,' I kid myself. As St Augustine said, 'Oh God, make me chaste, but not yet.'

Tebbit Test Revisited

July 2016

The Summer of 2011 was a sad time for a Pakistan cricket follower to write a book. I ended the Tebbit Test with a chapter on Shattered Dreams. I spoke of corruption being endemic and said that unless the administration was sorted out first you can't expect any lasting improvement. I suggested a period of isolation to purge the game.

It didn't happen but thank God it didn't. Instead the fear of being ostracised has led to reform There is now in place an effective administration led by a credible bunch of people.

But the biggest change is in nature of the team. Over five years it has been transformed from a bickering, quarrelling bunch of cheats team into a cohesive unit. They travel well, have an exceptional record. They have returned to England, to the scene of the spot-fixing scandal with a clean image. They are ranked third amongst Test teams and could well move to runner up spot by the end of the tour.

The credit for this goes to the captain MIsbah-ul-Haq. Yet thePakistani public has been grudging in their praise. Too dour, too humourless. They'd much rather have Shahid Afridi. I can understand people falling for flawed geniuses but who wants a flawed mediocrity,who's not just a cheat but a stupid cheat.

Have Pakistan changed for the better : am I willing to reverse my decision and start viewing a Pakistan supporter?

Th answer to the second part of the question is 'Yes.' The answer to the first part is more guarded. It has changed for the better but time will tell whether it is permanent.

We have reinstated Mohammcd Amir. Soon there may be pressure to do the same for Salman Butt and Mohammaed Asif. The latter has form. I would be extremely disappointed if either of them was reinstated.

Icki Iqbal

Acknowledgments

First of all I'd like to thank my daughter Deena for encouraging me to stick to my normal writing style. Next, I'd like to thank my wife Kadeeja whose scepticism acted as a spur and who eventually said, 'Why don't you write something about cricket?' although this book was not what she had in mind. I'd also like to thank Helen White's Creative Writing Group of Cobham, Surrey, Hilary Johnson's Authors Advisory Service and several other friends who have provided candid and constructive criticism of this and other works. To single out some might upset others but I must especially thank Jenny McNulty, David Holland, Ian Clark, Steve Shurety, Steve Little, John Treneman and Allen Kelly.

I list below books I have quoted from or relied on.

Ahmed, Mushtaq, *Twenty20 Vision*
Ahmed, Qamar, *Waqar Hassan*
Akram, Wasim, *Wasim*
Amarnath, Rajinder, *Lala Amarnath, The Making of a Legend*
Benaud, Richie, *Anything but an Autobiography*
Bradman, Don, *Farewell to Cricket*
Brearley, Mike, *The Art of Captaincy*
Baloch, Dr Khadim Hussain, *Summer of Swing*
Baloch, Dr Khadim Hussain, *The Hunt for Peace*
Baloch, Dr Khadim Hussain and Pervez, Mohammed Salim, *The Encyclopaedia of Pakistan Cricket*
Butt, Qamaruddin, *Cricket Without Challenge*
Butt, Qamaruddin, *Cricket Wonders*
Butt, Qamaruddin, *Pakistan Cricket on the March*
Butt, Qamaruddin, *Pakistan on Cricket Map*
Butt,, Qamaruddin, *The Oval Memories*

Butt, Shujauddin, *From Babes of Cricket to World Champion*
Butt, Shujauddin and Pervez, Mohammed Salim, *The Chequered History of Pakistan Cricket*
Chalke, Stephen, *At the Heart of English Cricket*
Close, Brian, *I don't Bruise Easily*
Crace, John, *Wasim and Waqar*
Fingleton, Jack, *The Greatest Test of All*
Frith, David, *The Bodyline Autopsy*
Graveney, Tom, *Cricket Through the Covers*
Hamilton, Duncan, *Harold Larwood*
Hayter, Peter, *Great Tests Recalled*
Hill, Alan, *Bill Edrich*
Kardar, A.H., *Green Shadows*
Kardar, A.H., *Inaugural Test Matches*
Kardar, A H, *Memoirs of an All Rounder*
Kardar, A H, *Test Status on Trial*
Khan, Imran, *All Round View*
Mahmood, Fazal, *From Dusk to Dawn*
Mailey, Arthur, *10 for 66 and All That*
Miandad, Javed, *Cutting Edge*
Mohammed, Hanif, *Playing for Pakistan*
Mohammed, Mushtaq, *Inside Out*
Noman, Omar, *Pride and Passion*
Oborne, Peter, *Basil D'Oliveira*
Perry, Roland, *Keith Miller*
Sandford, Christopher, *Imran Khan*
Singh, Jaswant, *Jinnah India Partition Independence*
Titmus, Fred, *Talk of the Double*
Warne, Shane, *Shane Warne's Century*
Wilde, Simon, *Caught*
Wisden, 1949–2011
Wolpert, Stanley, *Jinnah of Pakistan*

I have quoted from the lyrics of the Hindi song *Sub kuch seekha hamne na seekhi hoshiari* from the film *Anari* (Shailendra, Shankar-Jaikishen). I also borrowed a joke from Arthur Mailey's book listed above.

Helen White's Creative Writing Group &
Headless Chickens Creative Writing Group
Met regularly at Cobham Village Hall
Icki Iqbal, a member of both, wrote
The Tebbit Test there